The only step-by-step guide

AGED

VAL NIGOL

Published by Litehouse Books, 2016
PO Box 762
Kew Victoria 3101
agedcarebook.com.au
Copyright © Val Nigol 2016
Cover design and typesetting: workingtype studio
Cover photographs: depositphotos
Editor: Anthea Wynn
Line drawings: alifstyle
Printer: IngramSpark

National Library of Australia Cataloguing-in-Publication entryCreator:
Nigol, Val, author.
Title: Aged care: the complete Australian guide / Val Nigol.
ISBN: 9780987106643 (paperback)

Subjects: Older people--Care--Australia.
Older people--Services for--Australia.
Older people--Home care--Australia.
Older people--Housing--Australia
Old age homes--Australia

Dewey Number: 362.60994

While every effort has been made to ensure the reliability of the information presented in this book, neither the Publisher nor the author guarantees the accuracy of the data contained herein. Each reader should verify the data for themselves. Inclusion of any organisation, company, institution, publication, service or individual in this publication, does not imply endorsement by the Publisher.

All rights reserved. This book is copyright. Apart from any use as permitted under the Copyright Act 1968 no part of this publication may be reproduced, stored in a retrieval system or transmitted in any form or by any means, electronic, mechanical, photocopying, recording or otherwise, without the prior consent of the copyright holder.

The moral right of the author has been asserted.

To all those unsung,
unpaid and
under-paid heroes,
our current and future carers

Contents

Preface		1
Chapter 1:	Starting point	3
Chapter 2:	myagedcare gateway	7
Chapter 3:	At-home care	15
Chapter 4:	ACAT assessment	23
Chapter 5:	Home Care Packages	29
Chapter 6:	When to move	51
Chapter 7:	Residential homes	61
Chapter 8:	Finding a home	81
Chapter 9:	Moving in	103
Chapter 10:	The first weeks	113
Chapter 11:	Ongoing practical issues	121
Chapter 12:	Ongoing care concerns	141
Chapter 13:	Dementia	155
Chapter 14:	Fees and charges	167
Chapter 15:	Assets and income	187
Chapter 16:	Family home	197
Chapter 17:	Doing the sums	211
Chapter 18:	Other financial considerations	217
Chapter 19:	Financial strategies	225
Chapter 20:	Resources	241

Preface

This book is intended to be a one-stop shop. A step-by-step guide to the process of accessing and maximising aged care whether that is in your own home or in residential care. It has been written for you, the carer and/or the care-receiver and has been designed to dip in and out of as the need arises. To that end it has been structured in four parts:

- Part 1 talks about at-home care,
- Part 2 looks at residential care,
- Part 3 discusses the finances, and
- Part 4 provides information sources and a glossary of terms.

The word 'Mum' has been used throughout to signify the care-receiver. This is primarily to make the book easier to read but none of this is intended to preclude or offend Dad, other relations or friends, or couples. If the English language had a word for a gender-neutral elder which implied dignity and respect, then I would have used that word instead. The anecdotal stories are all true but some names have been changed to protect individual privacy.

Over time things will change, particularly the financial details. For the most up-to-date information, you should check the appropriate websites or with Centrelink. For financial issues

I strongly recommend that you consult Centrelink and/or an independent financial adviser who specialises in this area. For legal issues you should seek the appropriate professional advice.

Where medical information has been given, the quotes are from experts. If this material raises any queries or issues for you, then I suggest that you consult an appropriate medical practitioner. The financial advice comes from a qualified specialist and the practical processes have been enhanced by the experiences of aged-care experts.

Lastly this book has been written independently of any organisation or sector in the aged-care industry.

Val Nigol
August 2016

Chapter 1:
Starting point

You've just received the dreaded, but long expected phone call. 'Yes, it's Mum... she's had a fall. Yeah... bad. Broken her leg.'

You know what this really means. That Mum can't live at home on her own any more without a lot of extra help. Whether this means more help at home or having to find a care home remains to be seen but either way you, as her main carer, would be well advised to start finding out as much as you can about the processes and the costs of either path. By doing this ahead of the immediate need, you are investing in your own peace of mind as well as the best outcome for Mum.

So what are Mum's options once she has recovered? Broadly speaking they are probably one or some of the following and this combination might change over the longer term:

- downsize into a retirement community,
- help at home to varying degrees as needed,
- residential care home, and
- short-term respite care may be an additional option.

Although downsizing is outside the scope of this book, at this stage it is important to take a long-term view if you can. Increasing numbers of retirement communities offer ageing-in-place which provides the option to move to higher levels of care on the same premises. This means less upheaval for both her and the family later on and her friends will still be nearby.

At this stage too, you would be well advised to seek advice from a specialist aged-care financial adviser even if Mum's needs are relatively simple. The financial calculations for aged-care services are complex and interwoven with the Centrelink/DVA pension rules so that any short-term decisions could have unforeseen long-term consequences including tax implications. At a minimum have a look at Part 3 of this book but even with these insights, trying to work out the optimal route for Mum's personal circumstances is really a job for a professional.

When you are ready to initiate the process of getting government subsidised services then start by exploring the myagedcare website (see Chapter 2). This is the single entry point for every government subsidised aged-care service and it co-ordinates all care options including those that were previously run independently of each other. When you are ready to proceed then phone them at their Contact Centre.

Carers

Let's acknowledge these stalwarts of the system. Sometimes unpaid family members who take on this role are taken for granted and are almost invisible. They can find that their own health, career or education, finances and even family suffer in the process of looking after Mum, often with long-term consequences. Their contribution is often unrecognised by the community although the Australian Government is increasingly offering financial and practical support through its carer-gateway website at **carergateway.gov.au/**. The *Carer Recognition Act 2010* is also being phased in over the ten years following its introduction. Sources of support for carers are listed in the Resources in Part 4.

Before you look at the government's aged-care schemes, you need to consider whether care can be provided by the family or friends in the home. If Mum's needs are relatively simple, then most families will gradually and almost instinctively start down this path. These informal arrangements make an important contribution to the aged-care system and the carer may be entitled to receive government payments. The more common carer payments are these.

Carer Allowance

Centrelink recognises the daily care provided to a person at home with a disability, a medical condition or a frail older person, even if the carer works or is studying. The allowance provides fortnightly income support payments and is not subject to Centrelink's income or assets test thresholds. Care must be for a minimum of twelve months (or permanent) unless Mum has been told that she is likely to die in less than six months or she actually passes in that period. She must also meet certain levels of minimum care needs.

Carer Payment

This is a Centrelink payment designed to provide fortnightly income support if the carer is unable to work because of the demands of their caring role for a person with a severe disability, medical condition or who is frail and aged. Constant care must be given in the care-recipient's home.

The payment is at Centrelink age pension rates. Mum and the carer must both meet the age pension income and assets test thresholds and must be Australian residents. The care arrangement must be for at least six months (or permanent) unless Mum has been told that she is likely to die in less than six months or she actually passes in that period. In this case the carer will still be entitled to receive the carer payment.

The payments will cease if Mum moves into permanent residential aged care.

Carer Supplement

Centrelink can make an annual lump sum payment to a carer to assist with the cost of caring for a person and you might qualify if you receive a Carer Allowance or Carer Payment.

Chapter 2:
myagedcare gateway

> 🖥 **myagedcare.gov.au**
> ☎ **1800 200 422**
> **8am – 8pm Monday to Friday,**
> **10am – 2pm Saturdays**

There are three types of aged care available through the government system:

- Basic support in your own home. This is called the Commonwealth Home Support Programme (CHSP) and it offers a range of services covering domestic help, personal care, social support and allied health services.
- More complex support in your own home. This is called a Home Care Package (HCP) and it provides all of the same services as a CHSP but in a co-ordinated manner.
- Residential aged care where Mum moves permanently into a care home which provides for all her needs when she is unable to continue independently in her own home.

You can only access these programs through the Australian government's myagedcare gateway either through its website or by phoning its Contact Centre. Unless Mum is a DVA client (in which case she has to access to all the same facilities through the DVA) then this gateway is now the single and only place that you can access any of the services. This is irrespective of whether Mum only needs a podiatrist once a month right through to needing a secure residential home for advanced dementia.

The following diagram is intended to guide you through routes of the most popular parts of the myagedcare system. The abbreviations are explained in this chapter and are in the Glossary at the end of the book.

Part 1 — getting assessments done:

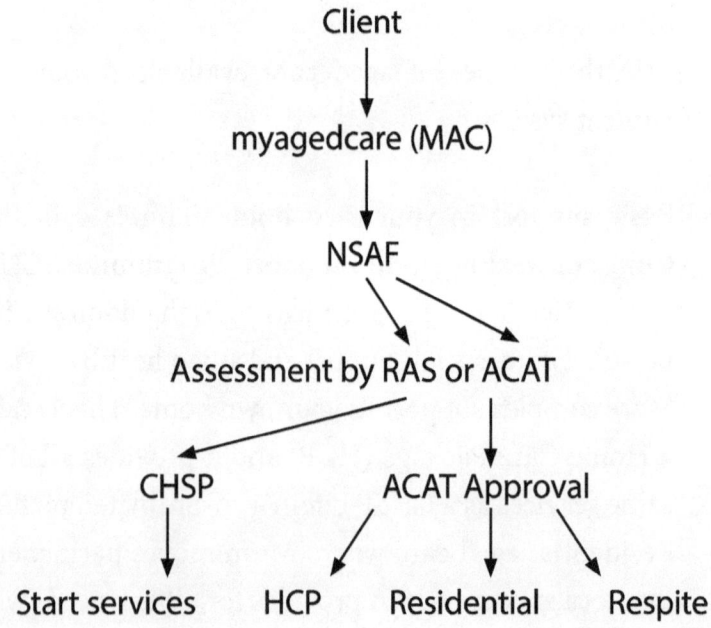

Part 2 — finding a provider and getting the financials sorted out:

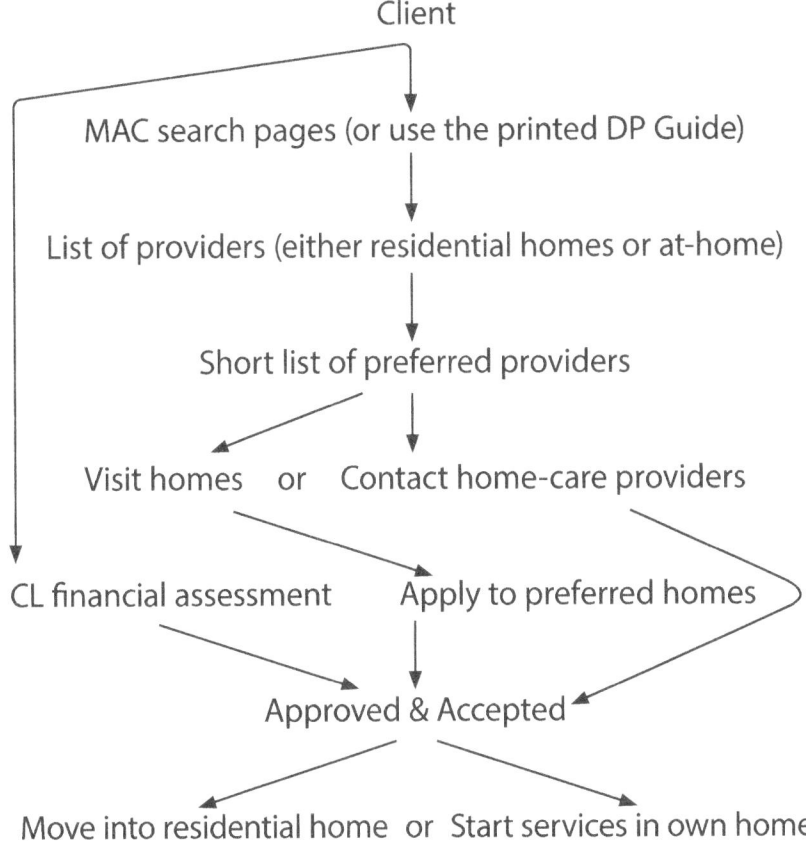

The MAC website is designed to help you with all aspects of aged care. It is an in-depth source of information with details about the different types of services, the eligibility criteria and the likely costs of accepting any of these services. It also has search mechanisms to help you find a service provider in your area regardless of whether you are looking for residential care homes or at-home care. If you do not have access to a computer or are not computer-savvy, then you can ring them for the same range of services.

When you first ring the Contact Centre they will ask for your permission to set up a personal client file (called the National Screening and Assessment Form or NSAF) which is designed to provide centralised and standardised screening for all levels of care needs. You won't have to repeat yourself every time you contact them.

In due course if you want to access this file you can do so by setting up an account (or using your existing account) at myGov (**my.gov.au**) and going to the Aged Care portal.

The myagedcare website itself is designed in gentle colours and uses a larger font so that it is easy to read. The topics are explained in simple English without being patronising and they are all delivered in in manageable-sized chunks. They are often illustrated with individual's stories. All the forms you will need are also here and can be downloaded.

It has a search bar at the top so if you don't quite know the correct phrase, you can use this to find all the possibilities. It also has search pages for finding an ACAT office, providers of at-home services or residential homes in your preferred area.

As a step towards greater transparency all residential homes, including non-subsidised ones, must now be listed on this website. They must all publish their maximum entry payments (which have replaced bonds) and they must keep these figures up to date. Any adverse care issues against a provider (for either at-home care or a residential home) are also published on the site so you can immediately get an up-to-date picture.

The one thing that is not co-ordinated through this gateway is the financial assessment that Mum will need for accessing some at-home care and any residential care. This is still done through

Centrelink. Although there is a fees estimator on the website, there are no clear guidelines about what should or should not be included.

> **Renato's story**
>
> As a financial adviser, I am fairly comfortable with using the myagedcare website but my advice is this. It is easy to use if you know how Centrelink/DHS assess different assets and types of income. There is no guide as to how you should enter data, what DVA payments to include, whether the Centrelink supplements should be included as income, how to include superannuation pension receipts or how to treat rental income. Without some detailed knowledge it would be difficult to get a correct estimate of the aged-care fee prior to making a decision about the affordability of these fees.
>
> **Lesson: The website is a convenient way to double check aged-care fee assessment letters but do not use it initially to work out aged-care fees which you will rely on to make the best financial decision.**

People with special needs

The legislation underpinning the whole aged-care system and therefore the myagedcare gateway is the *Aged Care Act 1997* and its more recent updates in the *Aged Care (Living Longer Living Better) Act 2013*.

Irrespective of the type of care you or Mum need, there are a number of groups who are defined in the *Aged Care Act* as having special needs. The full range of aged-care services must be available to all these groups:

- people from Aboriginal and Torres Strait Islander communities,
- people from culturally and linguistically diverse backgrounds,
- people who live in rural and remote areas,
- people who are financially or socially disadvantaged,
- veterans,
- people who are homeless or at risk of becoming homeless,
- people who identify as lesbian, gay, bisexual, transgender or intersex,
- people who are care leavers — people who were in institutional care (including foster care) as a child or young adult (or both) at some point in the 20th century. This includes Forgotten Australians and former child migrants who received a government apology in November 2009, and
- parents separated from their children by forced adoption or removal.

(From the Department of Social Services' *Five steps to accessing a Home Care Package.*)

Although people living with dementia are not defined in this list, all care providers are expected to be able to cater for their specialist needs.

PART 1

At-home care

Top Tips for at-home care

- Stay in your own home as long as possible with the benefits of at-home care.
- Ask the family how much support they can realistically give.
- Could you move in with the family while you are receiving at-home care if the need arose?
- If you are a home-owner, get financial advice before you complete your aged-care income assessment form.
- Get your ACAT assessment done before you need it; it doesn't expire.
- Once you have your ACAT approval don't ever lose the original paperwork; make copies for potential providers.
- If you move to another area your Home Care Package moves with you although you will have to find another provider.

Chapter 3:
At-home care

> **Information sources**
>
> 💻 **myagedcare.gov.au** ☎ 1800 200 422
> Complaints: ☎ 1800 200 422
> Advocacy: ☎ 1800 700 600

The post-war baby-boomer bulge in the Australian population is starting to need support services at an ever growing pace. The aged-care system now has an emphasis on helping people remain in their own homes longer by providing additional, subsidised, at-home care services. There has been significant growth in the number of Home Care Packages in recent years and these are expected to increase by approximately 80,000 over the next ten years.

A package is a personalised combination of home-help services to ensure Mum's ongoing safety and well-being. It might include domestic services, basic home maintenance or clinical therapy services. This mixture can vary in line with her changing needs.

At-home care can be delivered wherever Mum is living; it is not restricted to the traditional, suburban family home. If she has moved to a retirement village, an over-55s lifestyle community or even a caravan park then she is still eligible to receive this support — but not if she is in a residential care home. There is no minimum age requirement but all packages are designed for frail older people.

Today's big picture

In 2014, over 83,000 people across Australia received at-home care, two-thirds of whom were females and 20% of whom were aged over 90. Service providers from the not-for-profit sector contributed 80% of these services.

In the same period the government spent $5bn on at-home care and while this sounds a huge amount, a lot of it goes on the administration of the system often leaving less for the service recipients. Each provider will be allocated a certain number of Home Care Packages and once their client list equals the number of slots they have been given, they are unable to accept any new clients.

This can only change when a client leaves or the provider gets an increase in their allocation the following year. This might mean that they can't supply the particular services that Mum needs or that they can only offer them less frequently than perhaps she might like. A client would usually leave only because they have moved into residential care, they have died or affordability becomes an issue.

There are two home-care subsidies available namely:

- Commonwealth Home Support Programme (CHSP) or
- Home Care Package (HCP).

CHSP is a low-level program designed for those people who need help with just one or two services. If Mum's needs are more complex, then the co-ordinated HCP is the way to go. If she is a DVA client then the same range of services is available through the DVA.

CHSP services

CHSP is the entry-level service designed to assist both Mum and you as the carer, with daily living support to enable her to stay in her home longer. If Mum can answer yes to these three questions then she should apply for a CHSP:

- is she 65 or older (or 50 years or older and identifies as an Aboriginal and/or Torres Strait Islander person)?
- is she still living in her own home?
- does she need help to continue living independently?

To access these services you or Mum need to phone the myagedcare Contact Centre. They will arrange for an assessment of her needs. If these are relatively simple then a Home Support Assessment will be carried out by a member of the Regional Assessment Service (RAS).

CHSP can provide support both in the community and at home. The full range of services is listed on the myagedcare website but the most popular ones are:

- domestic help like cleaning, gardening, washing and ironing, shopping,
- personal care like help with showering and toileting,
- meals through meals-on-wheels or similar schemes,

- home maintenance like minor repairs around the home or garden,
- home modifications like installing safety aids such as alarms or ramps,
- transport for shopping or to get to appointments,
- nursing care for minor needs like dressing wounds,
- health-support services like physio or podiatry.

Community-based services may include:

- centre-based day care providing social activities in a community-based setting,
- meals served in a community centre.

(From the Department of Social Services'
Five steps to entry into an aged care home.)

Once Mum has been approved for a CHSP she will receive a letter confirming this. You can then use the search facility on the myagedcare website to generate a list of local providers in Mum's area. Be alert to the fact that private providers (those not subsidised by the government) may also show up on these lists and this is indicated by a tick or a cross in the last column of the details. You can arrange the details so that the subsidised providers all appear first.

All service providers are required to support people with special needs (see Chapter 2) as well as people from linguistic and culturally diverse backgrounds and some providers specialise in these areas.

Fees are charged individually for each service such as a lawn-mowing visit, the number of meals-on-wheels provided or each podiatry visit, and are payable directly to the provider.

Financial hardship support is not available for CHSP services.

HCP services

HCP is a significant expansion in government funding for subsidised at-home care. It is designed to help frail older people remain at home for as long as possible even when their care needs increase. It also gives Mum more control over the types of services she receives. The range is the same as the CHSP but they are provided as a co-ordinated package.

Before she can start an HCP, Mum will need an ACAT assessment (see Chapter 4) and she must be assessed as having basic care needs as a minimum.

Mum will be expected to make a financial contribution towards her services and this will vary depending on the nature of the services. She will have to pay a basic daily care fee plus an income tested fee. Full details of these are given in Chapter 5.

Home Care Standards

Although the providers may only be delivering one or two services on a weekly or fortnightly basis, they are still required to conform to a set of standards that are defined in legislation. Under the Home Care Standards, service providers need to:

- tell Mum about the services she will receive,
- tell her about any changes to these services,

- respect her privacy and dignity, and
- treat her concerns or complaints fairly and confidentially.

(From the Department of Social Services'
Five steps to accessing a Home Care Package.)

The Standards also ensure that Mum is able to have someone speak on her behalf (an advocate) in the case of any concerns or complaints.

If you or she feels that the provider is not meeting these standards or if you have any other concerns, then you should first discuss the problem with them. If you have persevered for a suitable period and you still feel that your issues haven't been addressed then you can ask for help from:

- Aged Care Complaints — a free service which investigates concerns about the health, safety or well-being of people receiving aged care.
- National Aged Care Advocacy Program — funds the state-based aged-care advocacy services.

Complaints can be lodged over the phone, on-line or in writing (details below).

Sanctions

A sanction is a government-imposed action against a residential care home or a home-care provider for non-compliance with the Standards. It can be applied when there is a serious problem with the care they deliver through either an aged-care home or a Home Care Package. Sanctions require the provider to fix the identified problem as quickly as possible. A sanction can be applied in two circumstances:

- when there is an immediate and severe risk to the health, safety or wellbeing of someone receiving care, or
- where a provider has been notified of Non-Compliance and has not fixed the problem.

Details of current sanctions are shown as part of each service provider's details on the myagedcare website.

More information

- myagedcare: **myagedcare.gov.au** or **1800 200 422**
- Commonwealth Home Support Programme: **myagedcare.gov.au/aged-care-services/commonwealth-home-support-programme**
- Home Care Package: **myagedcare.gov.au/aged-care-services/home-care-packages**
- Services provided: **myagedcare.gov.au/help-home**
- Find a provider: **myagedcare.gov.au/service-finder?tab=help-at-home**
- Standards for home care: **myagedcare.gov.au/financial-and-legal/rights-and-responsibilities-home-care**

- National Aged Care Advocacy Services: **1800 700 600** or **myagedcare.gov.au/how-make-complaint/advocacy-services** or **dss.gov.au/our-responsibilities/ageing-and-aged-care/older-people-their-families-and-carers/aged-care-advocacy**
- Aged Care Complaints: **myagedcare.gov.au/financial-and-legal/how-make-complaint** or **1800 200 422**
- Complaints fact sheets: **agedcarecomplaints.gov.au/resources/factsheets/**

Chapter 4:
ACAT assessment

> **Information sources**
> 💻 myagedcare.gov.au ☎ 1800 200 422

ACAT stands for Aged Care Assessment Team — in Victoria it is known as ACAS (Aged Care Assessment Services) but it means the same thing. Its purpose is to help families determine both the level and the type of care (whether at home or residential) that Mum needs. The assessment is free and is universal across Australia. A list of local ACATs is given in Part 4 of this book or you can use the ACAT finder at **myagedcare. gov.au/service-finder?tab=assessment-team.**

The assessment may be done either at home or in hospital if Mum has already been hospitalised. It is undertaken by a member of a team of medical specialists which can include doctors, physios, occupational therapists, social workers, nurses and psychologists. The nominated assessor will be the person who is best qualified to assess Mum's needs, so that if Mum is living with dementia for instance, then the assessor might be a psychologist. The process determines three things:

- the level of care Mum that needs,
- the amount of government funding that will be granted to partly pay for her care, and
- the approval will enable her to access subsidised residential care, a Home Care Package and/or respite care.

During the assessment, Mum has the right to:

- be treated with respect and dignity,
- receive information about the process, be told what is happening and why,
- express her own views, opinions and concerns,
- have someone with her during the assessment,
- have an interpreter present if that is needed, and
- have an independent advocate (who may be a carer or other family member or friend) help her with advice or to act on her behalf.

Assessment at home

Almost anyone can request an assessment. Mum can refer herself or you can ask on her behalf. It is a relatively simple process — contact the myagedcare Contact Centre by phone or online. They will create a centralised personal record for her. Mum's answers to their questions will help them decide what type of assessment she needs and is eligible for.

The ACAT assessment process will take around an hour during which time the assessor will ask questions about Mum's circumstances and needs, as well as some medical history. These are designed to work out how much and what type of help she needs with daily and personal activities. If more medical detail is necessary then, with Mum's approval, the ACAT team will also contact her doctor. Any special needs, like dementia, will be taken into account.

> **Jack's story**
>
> Jack's daughter arranged for an ACAT assessment to be done at home. Unfortunately she wasn't able to be present for the appointment. When the results arrived some weeks later she was surprised to see that Jack was assessed as not being eligible for a care package.
>
> She investigated and found that during the assessment Jack, who was fiercely independent and in denial about his needs, had answered the assessor's questions as if he was thirty years old and totally fit.
>
> **Lesson: The assessment has to be answered honestly with a realistic understanding of the situation.**

The team members may take several weeks to process the assessment during which time they will consult with their colleagues and possibly Mum's doctor. Their recommendations will be sent to the person who signed the assessment form.

Assessment in hospital

This may be co-ordinated by a social worker after the hospital's medical team has identified that this as the best way forward. The process is largely as described above — Mum's medical history (particularly her current hospital records), family circumstances and her needs will be the main considerations but she still has all the rights listed above. The family will also be consulted as part of the process. Because the hospital will want Mum's bed freed up as soon as possible, the result is likely to be determined within a day or two.

The outcome

The outcome of the assessment will determine the type of care that Mum needs. The possibilities are residential care or care in her own home, either of which may be coupled with respite care. If she is in hospital then transition care may be an interim option. If she has improved since the assessment and you feel she would be safe remaining at home, you have the added option of leaving things as they are. The assessment does not expire and Mum will only need a reassessment if she deteriorates so that her care needs have changed markedly.

> **Anthea's story**
> At 93 Mum was still managing adequately at home until one day she suddenly seemed to get depressed. Her doctor referred her for an ACAT assessment which was booked for several weeks ahead.
> In the meantime Mum perked up enough to ask why we were doing this assessment when she didn't need it! We went ahead with it anyway and the outcome was that residential care was not needed at this time. So we did nothing further about it. But we knew that it was on file as a benchmark for any future assessment.

> **Lesson: Managing Mum's situation is ever-changing. What is appropriate for today is not necessarily right for tomorrow.**

The ACAT paperwork is Mum's passport out of her current situation. It is really important that you do not lose it or give it away. Without it you cannot put her name on waiting lists for either at-home care or residential care. You should photocopy it and give these copies to potential homes or service providers. If you do lose it, then ring your ACAT office and ask for another copy. This paperwork achieves a number of things:

- it is valid across all Australian states and territories so that if you live in Queensland for instance but Mum is in South Australia, you can use it to find homes or providers near you,
- it does not expire so you are not obliged to rush off immediately and start the search, and
- if you use a placement service (see Chapter 8) to find a home, this enables them to proceed.

While ACAT centres can be a great source of information and support during your hunt, they cannot recommend any particular home or provider.

The final decision to go ahead with the ACAT's recommendation remains with Mum or you (or both). If you are not satisfied you should first contact your ACAT team leader. If this doesn't resolve the problem you should raise the issue with your state or territory Health Department, as each team is covered by their government's complaints procedures.

If you think that the outcome of the assessment is not appropriate then within twenty-eight days of receiving your approval, you can seek a review by writing to the Secretary of the Department of Social Services at:

The Secretary
Department of Social Services
C/- Director Aged Care Branch (NSW and ACT)
GPO Box 9820
Sydney NSW 2001

This service is free but there will be a fee if you progress the issue to the next level which is the Administrative Appeals Tribunal.

More information

- ACATs explained:
  myagedcare.gov.au/eligibility-and-assessment/acat-assessments
- Find your local ACAT team:
  myagedcare.gov.au/service-finder?tab=assessment-team
- ACAT concerns:
  myagedcare.gov.au/acat-assessments/concerns-about-acat-assessments

Chapter 5:
Home Care Packages

> **Information sources**
>
> 💻 myagedcare.gov.au ☎ 1800 200 422
> Complaints: ☎ 1800 200 422
> Advocacy: ☎ 1800 700 600

Consumer Directed Care (CDC)

All Home Care Packages (and from 2017 residential care) are founded on a philosophy called consumer-directed care which means that in theory you or Mum are in control of what services she wants and when they are delivered. This is achieved by the government paying the subsidies to the care-provider but Mum has control over how she spends them. This allows her to make choices about the types of care and services she receives and who will provide those services. She will be encouraged to identify her personal goals which could include wellness, independence and personal safety. These will form the basis of a legally binding Home Care Agreement and a care plan.

Mum will decide how much involvement she wishes to have in managing her package. This could range from participation in all aspects of it to a less active role in decision-making and its management. The provider should undertake ongoing monitoring and a regular re-assessment of the plan. This is to ensure that the package continues to meet Mum's needs which are likely to change as time goes on.

Suitability

A Home Care Package (HCP) provides the same range of services as the Home Support Programme but under an HCP these are co-ordinated because the recipient's needs are more complicated than someone who is only receiving a couple of services periodically. The rules for access are also more complex and interwoven but there are no restrictions on eligibility.

The easy way to be fairly certain that a HCP is appropriate for Mum is to ask her these questions. If she can answer yes to any of them, then you or she should go ahead and phone the myagedcare Contact Centre to progress this:

- is she an older person who needs some help to stay in her own home?
- is she finding some aspects of living at home hard?
- does she manage most of the time?
- does she think that if she doesn't get some help at home, she might have to go into an aged care home before she's ready?

A booklet called *Five steps to accessing a Home Care Package* is available from the myagedcare website to guide you through this process. A print version can be ordered or it can be downloaded. The five steps are:

- check Mum's eligibility,
- find an HCP provider,
- work out the costs,
- accept an HCP, and
- begin the services.

Checklist for a Home Care Package

		Date done	Completed
1	Contact myagedcare — a client record is set up Request an assessment		
2	Work out what services Mum needs		
3	ACAT assessment appointment made		
4	ACAT assessment done		
5	ACAT approval received		
6	Use myagedcare website to search for providers in your area. Make a composite list.		
7	Contact providers to check if they have availability		
8	Either make an appointment or put Mum's name on their waiting list.		
9	Follow-up the waiting lists periodically		
10	Work out the costs Use the estimator on the myagedcare website with care		
11	Accept a Home Care Package		

12	Check and sign the Home Care Agreement		
13	Develop a care plan with the provider		
14	Begin the services		
15	Review the plan periodically especially if Mum's needs change		
16	If you need to change the plan book an appointment with the provider		

(Derived from the Department of Social Services' *Five steps to accessing a Home Care Package*.)

Eligibility

The first step is arrange for Mum to have an ACAT assessment done (see Chapter 4). This can only be arranged through the myagedcare website. The assessment will define Mum's home-care needs at one of four levels which in turn will determine the amount of the government subsidy:

Home Care Package	Annual Government Subsidy
Level 1 Basic care needs	$ 7,924.15
Level 2 Low-level care needs	$14,417.50
Level 3 Intermediate-level care needs	$31,696.60
Level 4 High-level care needs	$48,183.65

Find a provider

Once Mum's ACAT has been approved, you should use the myagedcare website's search page to find providers in her area. You specify the level of care that Mum has been approved for and a list will come up on the screen. Be alert to the fact that private providers (those not subsidised by the government) may also show up on these lists and this is indicated by a tick or a cross in the last column of the details. Which one you use is totally your choice, so if possible contact several until you find one that Mum is happy with.

The provider will tell you whether they are able to supply the package Mum has been approved for. It may be that the provider has already used up their allocation of that particular package, so that neither they nor Mum will get any funding if they take her on. She can ask to go on their waiting list (or on several providers' waiting lists) without charge. Be aware that providers may accept new clients on a needs basis rather than a first-come-first-served basis. If Mum has been approved for a level 3 or 4 package, a provider may be able to supply a Level 1 or 2 package as a short-term interim solution.

Costs

Before Mum can accept an HCP, she will have to have an income assessment done. This is the one feature of getting aged-care services that is not accessed through the myagedcare gateway.

To explain the bureaucracy, the DHS sets the rules and costs and is responsible for the aged-care system, whereas Centrelink or the DVA are the organisations that assess Mum's assets and income on behalf of the DHS. The DHS then uses this information to work out her aged-care fees. Therefore it is essential that her Centrelink/DVA records are up to date so that they can calculate the correct fee.

If Mum is a Centrelink pensioner or is not a pensioner at all, her contact for aged-care assessment purposes will be through Centrelink. If she is a DVA client all her dealings will be through the DVA office in her state or territory.

You or Mum can progress this either through Centrelink or you can go to a specialist financial adviser who will do the sums and liaise with Centrelink for you. Alternatively you can complete the *Aged Care Fees Income Assessment* form (which is downloadable from **humanservices.gov.au/customer/forms/sa456**) and lodge it with Centrelink. If Mum is not a Centrelink pensioner she can chose not to complete this form but she will then have to pay the maximum fees.

There are two types of fees that Mum will be expected to pay, a basic daily care fee and an income tested fee.

The basic daily care fee is the same fixed amount for everyone and is currently $9.93 per day. These fees are indexed and increase on both 20 March and 20 September each year in line with Centrelink's age pension increases.

The income tested fee is based on her income and is calculated using a set formula. The current maximum fee is $14.25 per day. Mum's total cost will be the sum of both these fees and this figure will not be known until this latter one has been worked out.

There is a cost estimator on the myagedcare website. The webpages repeatedly use the word estimator because they can only give you a guide to the likely costs. As Renato's story in Chapter 2 shows, there are no guidelines about what figures should or should not be included here so to be safe, only take these figures as a broad guide.

Income tested fee

This is calculated using Mum's assessable income only; it ignores the value of her assets. Her assessable income is any money she physically receives from any of these sources including any Centrelink/DVA pension:

- salary, director's fees, business profits,
- superannuation schemes and allocated pensions,
- Government service pensions,
- Centrelink income support payments (excluding supplements),
- DVA pensions for veterans and widows without qualifying service (excluding supplements),
- overseas pensions,
- rental income, and
- compensation payments.

The next thing is that if Mum's assessable income falls below the following thresholds she will not have to pay any income tested fee. These thresholds have been set so that if she is receiving a full Centrelink age pension she will only have to pay the daily care fee.

- Single pensioner $25,711.40
- Member of a couple living together (combined) $25,243.40
- Illness separated couple (individual) $25,243.40

If Mum either receives a part age pension or she is not entitled to an age pension, there are two maximum levels of fees to help offset her longer-term costs. These are an annual maximum and a cumulative lifetime maximum and these levels currently are:

- Annual maximum for part-pensioners $ 5,187.97
- Annual maximum for non-pensioners $10,375.96
- Lifetime maximum $62,255.85

The amount of the income tested fee that Mum pays accrues against the lifetime maximum and this will apply regardless of how long she receives her HCP. It also continues on if and when she moves into residential care. In other words, you don't start counting from the beginning again once she moves; this cumulative figure spans from her first day with an HCP right through till she reaches this maximum. At this point she will no longer have to pay this fee and her care fees will reduce from then on. This also applies on a yearly basis to the annual maximum.

Let's work through an example so you can follow the logic. If Mum is a single pensioner needing a Level 1 HCP and her assessable income is $50,000, then her income tested fee will be calculated as follows:

1. Cost of care = $7,924.15 annum or $21.71 per day (this is the government subsidy)

2. Then the applicable threshold is deducted from her assessable income, so:
   $50,000 — $25,711.40 = $24,288.60

3. But only half this amount is used for this calculation, so:
   $24,288.60 / 2 = $12,144.30

4. Then the applicable annual maximum is added on, so:
   $12,144.30 + $5,187.97 = $17,332.27

5. Now divide this by 364 to get the daily rate, so:
   $17,332.27 / 364 = $47.69 per day

By these calculations Mum's daily rate of $47.69 is well in excess of the maximum income tested fee (which is $14.25) so she will only have to pay $14.25 per day.

Add to this Mum's basic daily care fee of $9.93 a day (or $3,624.45 per year) then her total costs for an HCP are:

$14.25 + $9.93 = $24.18 per day

Financial hardship

The Government recognises that not everyone can afford to pay aged-care fees and there are hardship provisions to ensure that Mum can still receive the care she needs either for an HCP or in an aged-care home. The fees and charges may be reduced or waived depending to her individual circumstances and the Government will pay some or all of these on her behalf.

This assistance is available to cover the basic daily care fee and/or income tested care fee provided she started receiving an HCP on or after 1 July 2014.

She will be granted hardship assistance if she finds herself in circumstances beyond her control, such as difficulties selling her home. It will not be paid if her difficulties are due to a choice or choices that she has made, such as giving away her assets. Equally she will not be eligible if she:

- is a self-funded retiree and has not completed and lodged an income assessment form,
- has gifted more than $10,000 in the previous twelve months, or more than $30,000 in the previous five years,
- has realisable assets valued at more than $34,082.10 (from March 2016).

Unlike the calculations for paying the income tested fee, normally for financial hardship assistance the value of her assets will be taken into account as part of the assessment process.

Accept a provider

Once Mum has found her preferred provider who has also agreed to accept her as a client, she should meet with them to discuss the care planning process. As part of this process she will have to agree the budget. All costs must be contained within the set budget which is held by the provider.

In this discussion Mum should include her own health goals and the level of control she wishes to exercise over the finances of her package and from that conversation the provider will draw up a care plan. This describes the types of care and services that will be provided and it will be formalised into a legally binding Home Care Agreement which will include details of:

- the types of services,
- who will provide which services,
- Mum's involvement in managing and coordinating the services,
- when and where the services will be delivered, and
- how much Mum will have to pay.

(From the Department of Social Services'
Five steps to accessing a Home Care Package.)

Package details

There are three types of services available — care, support and clinical services — and Mum can intermix them according to her personal needs.

- personal services: assistance with personal activities such as bathing, showering, toileting, dressing and undressing, mobility and communication.
- nutrition, hydration, meal preparation and diet: assistance with preparing meals including special diets for health, religious, cultural or other reasons; assistance with using eating utensils and assistance with feeding.
- continence management: assistance in using continence aids and appliances such as disposable pads and absorbent aids, commode chairs, bedpans and urinals, catheter and urinary drainage appliances, and enemas.
- mobility and dexterity: providing crutches, quadruped walkers, walking frames, walking sticks, mechanical devices for lifting, bed rails, slide sheets, sheepskins, tri-pillows, pressure relieving mattresses and assistance with the use of these aids.
- nursing, allied health and other clinical services: hearing services and vision services.
- transport and personal assistance: assistance with shopping, visiting health practitioners and attending social activities.

- management of skin integrity: assistance with bandages, dressings and skin emollients.

(From the Department of Social Services' *Five steps to accessing a Home Care Package.*)

The following additional services are also available with a government subsidy:

- veteran's supplement,
- oxygen supplement,
- enteral feeding supplement,
- viability supplement, and
- top-up supplement.

Begin the services

Technically Mum's package starts on the day she or you sign the Home Care Agreement which might be before or after the services have started. The HCP and the Agreement are valid for as long as she needs it and the government will continue funding it until such time as you or she tells the provider that she doesn't need it any more.

Over the longer term Mum's health may change. If these changes are not major then she can discuss them with her provider who should arrange a review of her care plan and its budget.

If however her needs change significantly, for example if she originally had low-care needs which have now increased to high care, then she or you should request that a new ACAT assessment is done to identify her new level of needs.

Mum can take a break from the services for any reason (which might include a stay in hospital or just to go on holidays) at any time and for any length of time as long as she or you have written to the provider telling them how long she will be away. If she has an emergency hospital admission you must tell the provider as soon as you can. In either case Mum and the provider should discuss what happens about her fees while she is away.

Mum will get regular monthly statements showing how the funds are being spent. A formal reassessment of the care plan and budget is conducted at least every twelve months. If at any other time she wishes to change the plan she is at liberty to discuss this with the provider who should accept her choices.

Lastly, if Mum moves to a new house in a different area, then she may need to find a new provider in her new district. She won't need a new assessment but the new provider will expect her to sign a new Home Care Agreement and work out a new care plan.

Claudio's story

Claudio's grandfather was living alone at home and receiving care services from a visiting home-care worker. This was provided by an agency which often meant that the same person would not be able to come each time. This was no reflection on the quality of care but rather that grandfather had got to know and like his regular carers. The real issue was that, like many older people living alone, he was lonely and a regular visitor who he knew became almost like a friend.

Now the other problem was that grandfather spoke very little English (he was Italian) and his regular carer was from south-east Asia and she had quite a strong accent. Communication eventually proved so difficult that either Claudio or his sisters had to visit each time to act as interpreter.

Lesson: Be alert to the possibility of communication problems like this, not just from language limitations but also from deafness.

Home Care Standards

Mum has a right to be looked after properly, treated well and given high-quality care and services. To make sure she gets the best care, all service providers have responsibilities and must meet certain standards. At the same time Mum too has some responsibilities towards her providers.

These Standards have been developed to simplify and standardise the way in which at-home care is delivered. Providers are required to meet set criteria in the areas of management systems and staffing, health and personal care, care recipient lifestyle, and physical environment and safety. This means that the provider needs to:

- explain the details of Mum's services to her,
- tell her about any changes to these services,
- respect her dignity and privacy, and
- treat any concerns or complaints fairly.

Charter of Rights and Responsibilities

The Charter acknowledges Mum's rights and those of her family and carers, as well as her responsibilities. According to the Charter, services should be delivered in a respectful manner. The Charter also says carers should be recognised as partners in care and be able to participate in decision-making in care situations when Mum is unable to. The Charter includes the right to:

- be treated with respect,
- be involved in deciding what care will meet your needs,
- have a written agreement covering everything you and your service provider have agreed to,
- have your care and services reviewed,
- have the privacy and confidentiality of your personal information respected,
- be given information on how to make comments and/or complaints about your care and services,
- have your fees determined in a way that is transparent, accessible and fair, and
- be given a copy of the Charter of Rights and Responsibilities for Home Care.

The Charter also outlines Mum's responsibilities, which means she needs to:

- respect the rights of care workers,
- give enough information to the service provider so they can develop and deliver her care plan,
- follow the terms and conditions of her written agreement,
- allow safe and reasonable access for care workers at the times agreed in her care plan, and
- pay any fees outlined in her written agreement.

(Copyright, Commonwealth of Australia; reproduced with permission.)

Advocacy and complaints

At any stage Mum can ask you or another person to help her or speak on her behalf in her dealings with the care provider. In the unlikely event that she has difficulty with this, then the National Aged Care Advocacy helpline is available (details below).

If Mum has any concerns about the nature, delivery or costs of her care plan then to start with, you or she should discuss it with the care provider. Usually the issue can be addressed quite easily and all providers must have a proper process for handling complaints.

If however this doesn't resolve the problem then you can contact Aged Care Complaints. This free service is available through the myagedcare website.

DVA clients

The same range of at-home support services is available for DVA clients but these are coordinated through the DVA. You or Mum should phone **133 254** or **1800 555 254** (for regional callers) for details or to request a service. The Veterans Home Care program provides domestic support, personal care, home and garden maintenance, respite care and social assistance.

Health support is available for a wide range of services and can be accessed by a referring letter from Mum's doctor. Co-payments are also in place for these services and the amounts are specific to the type of care provided.

More information

- myagedcare: **myagedcare.gov.au** or **1800 200 422**
- *Five Steps to accessing a Home Care Plan* booklet: **agedcare.health.gov.au/programs-services/home-care/five-steps-to-accessing-home-care-packages**
- Home Care Packages: **myagedcare.gov.au/aged-care-services/home-care-packages**
- Fee estimators: **myagedcare.gov.au/news/new-fee-estimators-assist-you-your-aged-care-costs**
- Find a local provider: **myagedcare.gov.au/service-finder?tab=home-care-package-providers**
- Home Care Agreement: **myagedcare.gov.au/aged-care-services/home-care-packages/home-care-agreement**
- Charter of Rights and Responsibilities: **health.gov.au/internet/main/publishing.nsf/Content/ageing-charter-rights.htm**
- National Aged Care Advocacy Services: **1800 700 600** or **myagedcare.gov.au/how-make-complaint/advocacy-services**
- Aged Care Complaints: **myagedcare.gov.au/financial-and-legal/how-make-complaint** or **1800 200 422**
- Low-income and homeless support from Wintringham Specialist Aged Care: **wintringham.org.au/home_care_packages.html** or **03 9034 4824**
- DVA Veterans' Home Care: **dva.gov.au/providers/provider-programmes/veterans-home-care**
- DVA health services: **dva.gov.au/health-and-wellbeing**
- DVA enquiries: **133 254** or **1800 555 254** (for regional callers)

PART 2:
Residential care

Top Tips for planning for residential care

- Advice from the Boy Scouts: Be Prepared! Arrange for a ACAT assessment to be done.
- Start looking at possible homes well in advance of needing one.
- Put your name on the waiting lists of all the homes that you like.
- As a member of a couple, decide if you both want to move together.
- Don't leave it too late to move; the adjustment phase is hard enough when you can still manage but after that it becomes really difficult.
- Start arranging your legal documents if you haven't already done so.
- If possible organise a short stay as respite care in your preferred home so you can 'try before you buy'.
- If you are a home-owner then this is the trigger for seeking professional advice about how to structure your finances. Don't just sell the house and then ask.

Top Tips for once you are in a home

- On day one, you are likely to be scared, anxious, frightened and totally out of your comfort zone; if you are vision or hearing impaired this will make it even worse.
- You won't get one-to-one care which you are likely to be used to at home.
- You are likely to be surrounded by residents with varying degrees of dementia which can be frustrating at first if you still have your mental capabilities.

Chapter 6:
When to move

We have all watched friends and relatives slowly deteriorate as they age. Unless we are directly involved in their care, we tend to distance ourselves from the situation, particularly as it becomes more demanding. However, for many carers the time eventually comes when they have to face up to the possibility of moving a loved one into residential care. This could equally be for reasons that the carer can no longer cope as much as it is due to Mum's deterioration. This can trigger all kinds of emotional responses as well as a catalogue of actions for the family.

Signs

Even though Mum might have a condition which is going to worsen over time, this isn't necessarily a trigger in itself. With increased help she may still be able to cope at home for some time to come. The decision to move is often triggered by an unexpected event, a fall or serious illness. The result may be that she's no longer physically safe at home on her own or she is unable to maintain her personal standards. Even with all the home-help she can get, she may no longer be able to manage the house adequately. There are a number of specific conditions that she might develop:

- increasing numbers and severity of falls,
- increasing difficulties with balance and walking,
- broken bones(s) as the result of a fall,
- pain management,
- worsening continence,
- challenging or disruptive behaviours, or
- deteriorating thinking, communication and memory.

Options

The short-term choices are going to be governed by Mum's immediate needs and the carer's and family's circumstances. Perhaps having some, or extra, help at home would make her situation manageable for the short term (in which case see the preceding chapters for how to go about this.) If that isn't viable then respite care or alternative family arrangements may be a workable solution.

It may be that a spell in respite gives Mum a much-needed break, and you as carer the chance to recharge your own batteries and reconnect to your own life. It can also happen that having now tasted the easier life in a home, Mum decides that she would like to stay. Whatever the outcome, respite is only an interim solution that creates an opportunity for you all to consider the longer term.

Jenny's story

After Dad went into residential care Mum was left on her own in the family home, insisting that she would never move into 'one of those places'. She had a series of skin operations on her legs, which gradually reduced her capacity to care for herself at home. After one operation, we placed her for respite at the same home as my father.

For the first week, she was quite resistant. We reassured her by telling her it was for medical reasons and that she would be going home in a fortnight. By the second week she liked it there and by the end she didn't want to leave. We knew then that we could move her with her consent. Her name had been down for five years, so when we told the home, they moved her to the top of the list. She moved in three weeks later.

Lesson: It's really important to get Mum to buy into the decision and what better way than try before you buy.

Rate of decline

Mum's decline may be gradual or sudden, with the latter resulting from an unexpected illness or injury. While the resulting process of getting her into a home will be the same, the timescale for achieving a satisfactory outcome will be much more pressing when it is triggered by a sudden problem.

If the deterioration is gradual, it can be very hard to know at what point you should take that usually irreversible step of residential care. However, if it seems that Mum's situation is unlikely to improve, then the best advice is from the Boy Scouts: be prepared. Start doing your homework now — look into care homes, make your lists of criteria for the home, start an assessment of Mum's financial position and get an ACAT assessment done. Start discussing the options with her and find out her likes, needs and wants. This can take some of the stress out of the situation if and when the time finally arrives.

However older people can perceive that this is the last straw when psychologically they are not ready to be 'bundled off to a home'. The reality is that ACAT assessments do not expire. If you decide to put Mum's name down on waiting-lists, then you are going to need the ACAT paperwork. It will reduce the pressure if the unexpected suddenly happens.

If Mum can be looked after at home then the time pressure to find a residential care solution is lessened. If, on the other hand, Mum is hospitalised and simply can't come home again, then there can be tremendous pressure on the family to make alternative arrangements. Understandably the hospital will want the bed vacated as soon as possible because hospital beds are intended for the sick not the aged.

Under these circumstances an ACAT assessment will define all the possible options both interim and long term. A move from hospital to transition care can be one way of gaining time in which to find your preferred home. If this isn't an option, then moving Mum into respite care can also achieve that time window for finding a more permanent solution.

How the system works

The very first thing that you should do is download (or order a print copy) of the booklet *Five steps to entry into an aged care home* which is available from the myagedcare website. This steps you through the process. After that you would do well to spend some time exploring this website because the process is probably not as simple as the booklet would like you to believe — as Renato's story in Chapter 2 explains.

After that a number of things can happen but not necessarily one at a time. If Mum lives with dementia then you will have to do it all for her. If not, then she can do some preparation at home while you are researching potential homes. But you should try and keep in mind that the choices and decisions should preferably be hers and they should be based on what is important to her. She should feel that she has ownership of the outcome. These steps are elaborated in the following chapters:

- Contact the myagedcare gateway to arrange for an ACAT assessment to determine the level of care Mum needs.
- Find a home after researching, visiting, short-listing and applying. Consider using a placement service to do it for you especially if you are interstate.
- Preparation at home includes deciding on what clothes, furniture and personal effects to take, making or updating a will, powers of attorney and a list for change of address.
- Financial assessment by either the DVA or Centrelink will determine the level of fees and charges she will have to pay.
- Financial advice from an independent expert will help Mum plan and manage these fees and costs and the long-term future for the family finances.
- Moving day might need a moving van to transport the furniture, set up her room and ensure that you have support after it is all over.

For details about how the ACAT assessment process works see Chapter 4. Once Mum has received her approval letter it will tell you what level of care she is eligible for. Her perception of this is can be that, 'I'm not ready to be bundled off to a home to die.' And along with that concern is the idea that she will be 'put away' tomorrow and will lose contact with her family and friends.

This means that one of the biggest demands on you is the ability to manage Mum's fears and expectations. She may not realise that the assessment does not expire which means that you have as long as you need to decide and move on to the next step.

Try explaining that taking this step is a positive thing because it creates options and opens doors to new possibilities that she wouldn't have otherwise. A whole new world awaits her out there...

Sam's story

Sam and his brother were still living at home when Grandma moved in which forced both Mum and Grandma to share a bedroom. This arrangement worked well enough and Grandma stayed for some years. One day Mum had a car accident which resulted in a lengthy hospitalisation. Grandma moved to her other daughter until it finally became necessary for her to move into a care home.

This was a situation the family had tried hard to avoid. However, they need not have worried. It soon became clear that Grandma was enjoying her new situation. She was no longer a guest in someone else's home, her room was her own and to personalise it she asked for her own possessions to be brought in. She fully accepted that her needs could now be best provided in aged-care accommodation.

Lesson: Contrary to many people's expectations, moving into a care home can be a liberating experience. Try and see the opportunities of the new situation.

Emotional support

This move is going to be a big project for everyone involved, but the main people needing support are going to be Mum and you the main carer.

You don't have to be too bright to realise that a move into residential care is frequently a one-way ticket. The person most acutely aware of this will be… Mum. It will be a topic of conversation amongst her friends and she will know people who have moved into one and she may well have friends who have passed while they were there.

Talking to her about it and getting her to agree can be a process demanding much patience, tact, diplomacy and sensitivity on your part. It can take time for her to accept the need for the move. Even if intellectually she understands that it is sensible, it doesn't mean that she is bubbling with joy at the prospect.

So try to treat her gently throughout the process but particularly at the outset. Have respect for her views, thoughts and perceived needs. The longer any of us have to accept a new idea, the more comfortable we become with it. Mum will usually want to be close to her family and friends and she will find it easier to make the move if she already knows someone in the home.

Mum's perspective

By the time Mum has reached the point of needing residential care, it may be that she has been living alone for some time. She may also be virtually house-bound or only able to get out for very short walks. The consequence of this is that her world has shrunk to the four walls of her house. This manifests in her conversation and priorities which have become limited to what others might consider to be life's minutia. You might get conversations in which for instance, she bemoans the fact that the post was five minutes late yesterday. This is now her world and we have to respect this.

Now you are proposing to upend this safe and known world and move her into a totally unfamiliar place which, in her mind, is filled with scary uncertainties. In the interim, while you are researching homes her current world will be topsy-turvy with all the new things she has to think about. She is likely to be in a continual state of anxiety.

The best way to lessen this is to take time, and lots of it, to explain to her what is happening, when and why. You may need to present ideas one at a time and slowly especially if her speed of mental processing and understanding is slower than it used to be. If her short-term memory is not so good either, you might have to repeat it a few times as well. Try putting yourself in her shoes — this may well help you to understand her position a whole lot better.

Family and carer support

You may have been the main or only carer, and for a long time, before being forced to face the decision about residential care. Being a solitary supporter can be a lonely responsibility so now is the time to rally the family and anyone else who is willing to help and support you in the coming weeks of decisions, planning and moving.

One way to do this is to have a support-group meeting, or series of them if necessary. This will enable you all to plan the move, share the practical tasks around the group and resolve any conflicts that might arise. If such a meeting is likely to be difficult or contentious then have it on neutral territory, a cafe perhaps, and nominate someone to run it. Some members of the group might find the whole subject distressing so the chairperson needs to be patient and empathic. If necessary get some practical tips from someone who regularly runs meetings.

Right from the start though, you need to be clear about who you are making the decision for. Is it really for Mum and in her best interests, or if you are being brutally honest, is it to make life easier for yourself and other family members? There is nothing wrong in declaring your own needs and interests. You also need to be aware that if Mum disagrees with the decision to go into a home, then nobody can force her.

Although the focus will be on Mum and getting her needs met, the carer will also need support. Often the carer is the partner/spouse or the single child with no family of his/her own. So make it a priority to find other family members or close friends who can be counted on to be there for you too. If you know someone who has been through it themselves, they are likely to be more understanding. If you don't get this support, your own health can suffer in the process, then you will be no help to Mum or yourself.

At various times, you are likely to experience a variety of emotions:

- have we made the right decision?
- guilt about 'deserting' Mum — it was my 'job' to look after her,
- relief or selfishness that you have now got your own life back,
- relief that you no longer have that responsibility,
- self-reproach,
- inadequacy because you couldn't cope at times,
- exhaustion and depression from the demands of the process,

- anger that the costs are a financial drain to your future detriment, or
- anxious that the money won't last the distance.

These are all normal reactions. Don't make it worse by beating yourself up because you are feeling like this.

Carer overload

Before Mum moves into a home, care-giving can be an unrelenting round of responsibilities, challenges, activities and demands. Once she is in, the responsibilities and demands will lessen but the time involved can still be considerable. Even more so if you are doing it solo. You need to keep an eye out for serious overload which can include (but are not limited to):

- feeling totally physically and emotionally drained and permanently exhausted,
- getting cranky, short-tempered or impatient,
- feeling depressed, resentful or helpless,
- smoking and/or drinking more than usual, or
- losing interest in everything else in your life.

Try to build in some time-out for yourself on a regular and frequent basis. This lets you relieve the built-up tension and also gives you space to mentally switch off from it all. If you are really struggling, then try talking to someone outside the family. There are Commonwealth carer resources whose primary focus is support. Details of these are listed in the Resources in Part 4.

Chapter 7:
Residential homes

> **Information sources**
> 🖥 myagedcare.gov.au
> ☎ 1800 200 422

Today's big picture

To give you some idea of the profile of aged-care homes and their residents in 2014, let's start by painting a picture of the Australian industry. While you may ask what this has to do with your own particular situation, having some broader understanding can give you an insight into the nature and structure of the homes even to the point of influencing your choices.

Firstly, over 270,000 Australians aged over 65 were in permanent residential care during 2014. This was 8% of the population. For a more detailed picture, the following figures are taken from the Australian Institute of Health and Welfare's *Residential age care and Home Care 2013-14*:

- male/female split: 31% male, 69% female

- women: 62% widowed, 22% married/de facto, 16% single/divorced
- men: 25% widowed, 45% married/de facto, 30% single/divorced
- ages: 77% were aged over 80, 33% were aged over 90
- main health reason for admission: dementia (67%)
- other admission reasons: 47% low care, 40% with complex care needs
- preferred language: 90% English
- country of birth: 69% Australia, 31% overseas
- reason for leaving: 78% death, 13% changing homes

Industry perspective

Although historically, residential aged care was provided by the churches and other not-for-profit organisations, by 2014 the shape of the industry moved on a long way:

- number of places: over 189,000
- number of homes: 2,688
- number of providers of homes: 1016
- homes with 60+ places: 50% (compared with 28% in 2004)
- providers: 57% not-for-profit, 5% government, 37% for-profit
- care offered: 60% high care only, 2% low care only, 38% mixed care

There have been, and continue to be, two major trends in the industry. The first is that for-profit companies see aged-care as a big opportunity and increasingly homes are moving into corporate ownership. The other aspect is that newly built homes are increasingly larger. When you appreciate that economies of scale will arise from operating larger homes, which in turn means lower costs and more profit, then this trend is almost inevitable.

Alongside corporate ownership comes the concern that profit is being forged at the expense of quality of care. The rude truth is that profit is the primary driver for all for-profit companies, irrespective of the industry sector, which in turn fuels their obligations to their shareholders. If Mum is moving into a corporately-owned home then you should keep alert for changes that might mean cost-savings to the potential detriment of the services or amenities.

However having said that, in 2015 the five largest providers of homes across Australia were (in order) BUPA, Estia, the Catholic church, the RSL and Blue Cross, the last three being not-for-profit organisations.

The 2016 Federal budget announced new measures which will result in lower government payments to aged-care providers. This then raises the question of the future viability of some providers and others consolidating through mergers.

There are several other changes that have continued unwaveringly for the last ten years, if not more:

- more places are available every year in line with the ageing population,
- the cost of providing care increases every year and not all homes are able to absorb these and still continue to operate, and
- the trend to fewer but larger homes. Between 2007 and 2014, the number of homes has dropped by 6% but the number of places has increased by 13%.

Types of homes and care

There is a range of types of homes and different levels of care provided by both accredited and private homes. Sometimes different words are used to describe the same type of care, just to confuse. So it is worth looking at these in some detail.

There are also a few other types of care which are available for specific situations. The first five of the following are only accessible once Mum has received her ACAT approval.

Permanent homes

Homes can provide one or more of the following types of accommodation:

- low-level care — personal and domestic care,
- high-level care — akin to nursing care and including low-level dementia, in addition to low-level care,
- dementia care — secure specialist facilities,
- extra services, or
- suites as well as single rooms.

In 2014 nearly 40% of homes offered mixed low and high care, whereas only 2% were low-care only. For all intents and purposes, Mum will not be aware of whether she is receiving low or high level of care; this has more to do with the amount of subsidy that the provider is receiving.

There is a growing demand for suites. This is accommodation that provides two adjacent interlinked rooms where one is the bedroom with its en suite bathroom and the other is a living room possibly with a kitchenette.

Dementia care

This is specialist care which caters for residents with high levels of dementia or other forms of mental or cognitive dysfunction. These homes will have specialist dementia-trained staff and higher levels of security. Residents receive the same care as provided in general homes plus additional dementia-related practices and services. Given that two-thirds of all new residents have dementia as their primary health problem, there are increasing numbers of dementia-care units available.

Extra services

Some aged-care homes choose to provide higher standards of accommodation, food and personal services for an additional daily fee. However, the level of care will be the same because all homes are obliged to provide this to the same standard. These homes are increasingly offering suites or double rooms. The single rooms may also be larger than normal.

Respite care

Respite is short-term care usually taken to recover from an injury or illness or to give the carer a break. Mum is entitled to up to nine weeks per year. Once she has her ACAT approval, she can book into respite without any medical need. This is a useful 'try before you buy' strategy to see if she can adapt to the lifestyle, although not all homes offer respite care.

If Mum needs respite on an emergency basis, then phone your local Commonwealth Respite and Carelink Centre on **1800 052 222** during business hours or **1800 059 059** outside business hours.

Transition care

Transition care is an intermediate, flexible, short-term residential service which could be available after a stay in hospital. Mum's ACAT approval will only valid be for four weeks. Transition care provides low-intensity therapy (such as physio or occupational therapy) and support as part of an ongoing recovery process. The aim is to help increase Mum's independence and confidence so that she can return home rather than going into a care home prematurely. If Mum needs a care home it gives you time to find one for her. The maximum stay is twelve weeks but this could be extended to eighteen weeks if needed.

Multi-purpose services

The Multi-Purpose Services Programme is a co-ordinated initiative specifically for rural areas. It combines all the health services giving each local community the flexibility to allocate its funding according to local health-care needs.

Supported residential services (SRS)

These are privately owned, permanent residential homes operating in New South Wales, Queensland, South Australia and Victoria which run alongside the national aged-care system. They are all registered and regulated by their state or local government. They do not receive any government funding nor do they have to meet the accreditation standards defined in the *Aged Care Act 1997*. In the other states and territories, all homes are part of the federal system. See the DVA's information database at CLIK for more information at **clik.dva.gov.au/ search/node?search_fulltext=supported+residential+services.** SRS generally only provide personal living services such as meals, laundry and cleaning, and not nursing services. Just because these homes are outside the mainstream of federal government-regulated homes does not mean that they provide a lesser standard of accommodation or facilities. They are generally run by owner-operators and the profile of residents can be younger and more active than in mainstream homes. You should assess them in the same way as you would any other home (see Chapter 8).

Victoria — has the largest number of SRS and in 2016 there were 135 registered homes largely in metropolitan Melbourne. They are regulated by the Victorian Department of Health under the *Supported Residential Services (Private Proprietors) Act 2010*. Fees and charges are not regulated and can vary from 85% of the pension to $1000 per week. See **www2.health.vic.gov.au/ageing-and-aged-care/supported-residential-services/information-for-residents** for more information.

Queensland — SRS here are regulated under the *Residential Services (Accommodation) Bill 2002* which covers accommodation for non-aged care situations as well. It regulates 'aged care accommodation units' which mostly appear to be independent living units or assisted living, (the terminology gets blurred), where the resident lives independently but there is 24-hour assistance at hand if necessary and communal facilities for activities and possibly meals.

South Australia — In 2013 there were around thirty SRS in South Australia but they provide care only for people with mentally-related problems ranging from dementia to brain injury. They also cater for people of all ages and you need to be assessed before you can be admitted. They are regulated by the *Supported Residential Facilities Act 1992* and the *Supported Residential Facilities Regulations 2009*. The Seniors Information Service has more details at **seniors.asn.au**.

New South Wales — The term SRS appears to have more than one meaning here. It can vary from a residential care home (in the sense of a federally funded and regulated home) to an independent living unit/villa/cottage/apartment (which you might also find in a retirement village) or a supported living unit (which is akin to a home providing personal care but outside the federal system).

Eden Alternative

The Eden Alternative™ is a different, more empathic model for providing residential aged care. It acknowledges that loneliness, boredom and helplessness are the most debilitating and limiting 'diseases' of old age and it seeks to rectify these by encouraging homes to incorporate animals and gardens into the everyday lives of its residents. Children are also encouraged to visit as another part of its philosophy.

The Eden Alternative is defined in its ten principles which can been seen on their website. If you think Mum would be happier in an Eden environment, then their website also provides a list of these homes throughout Australia although the majority are currently in Queensland.

Palliative care

End-of-life care (known as palliative care) in aged-care homes aims to give Mum the best possible quality of life, reducing the need to move her to another location such as a hospital or hospice. Palliative care uses a holistic approach to managing pain and other symptoms. It also addresses her physical, emotional, cultural, social and spiritual needs as well as those of the family and carers. It focuses on living well until death. All homes are required to provide palliative care.

What is provided

The infrastructure of a home and how it is run is largely dictated by the government's regulations. However, these can never dictate its look and feel, its soul. While it is impossible to get a total feel for a home until Mum has lived there for a while, there are some factors you should be aware of as you visit. Most of these are listed in the checklists in the Resources in Part 4 but it is worth adding to this.

Homes are now required to have a higher percentage of single rooms. Single rooms are great for providing privacy but they can also bring isolation. On the other hand, shared rooms can bring constant companionship provided you get along with your room-mate.

All homes must provide a specified range of care and services which will vary according to whether the resident has low-care or high-care needs. (The following lists are taken from **myagedcare.gov.au/living-aged-care-home/care-and-services-aged-care-homes**).

Accommodation services

All residents can receive specified care and services relating to:

- furnishings,
- bedding,
- cleaning services,
- waste disposal,
- general laundry,
- basic toiletries,
- all meals and refreshments,
- social activities,
- utilities,
- maintenance of buildings and grounds, and
- staff to provide emergency help.

Personal care and services

All residents have these services available to them:

- bathing and showering, dressing, grooming,
- assistance with eating,
- assistance with mobility,
- maintaining continence or managing incontinence,
- assistance with taking medication,
- access to health and therapy services,
- help with communication with other people,
- emotional support if needed,
- support for people with cognitive impairment, and
- Additional requirements for nursing care.

High-care residents must be provided with additional items, care and services such as:

- standard mobility aids like crutches or walking frames,
- incontinence aids,
- nursing services, and
- therapy services.

Because residential care is an increasingly competitive business, homes may offer additional facilities like a coffee shop on the premises (great for visitors), a cinema room with regular movie sessions, a private dining room with special meals periodically and a community bus for outings. Upmarket homes may have more luxury services like a concierge car service.

Costs

Although accredited homes are subsidised by the government Mum is also required to contribute. The amount and the structure of the fees are means tested at the outset and are adjusted twice yearly in line with the pension. Full details are given in Chapters 14 to 18 and ways to manage the fees and family finances are discussed at length in Chapter 19.

All the possible fees are shown below but Mum will only be faced with some of them depending on her circumstances and the outcome of her financial assessment:

- basic daily care fee,
- means tested fee,
- refundable accommodation deposit (RAD),

- daily accommodation payment (DAP),
- refundable accommodation contribution (RAC),
- daily accommodation contribution (DAC), and
- extra-services fee.

Who's who in a home

The first thing to realize is that there won't be just one person looking after any one resident. With at least three daily shifts of staff and people fulfilling different roles, there are a number of people you will have to get to know. Staff may wear uniforms in some homes but not in others and most will have name badges. In the beginning it can be confusing working out who is who. Broadly speaking there are two groups, the business/administrative people and the nursing/care staff.

Administrative staff

These people are usually only on-site in the home through normal or extended business hours.

- owners — these may be a not-for-profit organisation or a private company or even a big (sometimes international) corporation. The type of ownership will have a big impact on how many staff there are depending on their corporate policies.
- management — in small private homes, the administrative manager may also be the owner. In larger homes, the manager is likely to be an experienced aged-care

administrator. This person has the ultimate responsibility for the financial and administrative running of the home.
- management staff — this can include receptionists, office staff, book-keeping and accounting personnel.
- catering manager — or a senior cook as well as chefs/cooks depending on the size of the home. There will also be waiting staff who deliver the meals.
- laundry and cleaning staff.
- maintenance staff — this can include gardeners, maintenance people and any other specialist trades that might be required. They may be employed on a contract basis.

Nursing/care staff

- Director of Nursing (DON) — is the person with the ultimate responsibility for the residents' care and to whom all the nursing staff report. This person may also be known as the Director of Care. They must also ensure that all the care standards are met.
- nurses — there should be at least one registered nurse on every shift.
- carers — sometimes called personal carers or personal care assistants (PCAs). These are usually the majority of the staff and they undertake the tasks associated with the resident's personal care like showering and dressing. Their level of qualifications will determine how much help they can provide. Increasingly care staff are from overseas often speaking with distinct accents. If Mum has a hearing impairment then this can make communication more difficult.

- support staff — these can include some or all of physios, occupational therapists, social workers, counsellors, dieticians, hairdressers and podiatrists. These people are usually outside staff who come at set times or when there is a specific need.
- activities or lifestyle staff — there is likely to be a co-ordinator or manager who arranges all the activities, or there may be individuals with specific skills who come in to run certain activities — or both.
- trainees — work experience is mandatory for trainee aged-care workers and nurses; they generally stay for one or two weeks before moving on.

Agency staff

Many homes can only operate using agency and/or relieving nurses or carers. This might be due to financial limitations or the lack of local aged-care staff or even to cover a short-term illness, but also to match the numbers of residents and their level of care needs as these change.

If you are talking to a new nurse or carer who doesn't appear to understand Mum's situation, bear in mind they might be from an agency. If this is their first shift at Mum's home, they don't know the residents, the other staff, the physical layout, never mind the details of any one person's care needs. Remember what it was like on your first day in a new job? So be patient and explain your problem gently. This will help them to help you.

Communication with staff

As the main carer there will inevitably be times when you need to talk to a staff member. The question is, who? The best person to start with every time, is the person-in-charge and this may vary depending on the time of day or night. They can then delegate any tasks that need to be done to resolve any issues or care needs. If the issue is an on-going one, then they are also responsible for ensuring that the appropriate people on the next shift are aware of the situation.

All care homes are run by shifts of staff. These shifts vary in length with the night shift usually being the longest. When one shift ends and the next begins the staff will all meet to do a handover. At this time you may notice that there is no staff around the home.

Shifts usually change at 7am, between 3-4pm, and between 9-11pm. Some morning shifts can be shorter entailing a handover around 1pm. You are more likely to have a helpful conversation with the staff if you can avoid disturbing them at these times.

Resident's rights

Within Australia, the *Aged Care Act 1997* defines the rules and regulations governing residential aged-care homes. From this has come the following Charter of Residents' Rights and Responsibilities which homes should have on display for anyone to read. All residents have the right to:

- full and effective use of his or her personal, civil, legal and consumer rights,

- quality care which is appropriate to his or her needs,
- full information about his or her own state of health and about available treatments,
- be treated with dignity and respect, and to live without exploitation, abuse or neglect,
- live without discrimination or victimisation, and without being obliged to feel grateful to those providing his or her care and accommodation,
- personal privacy,
- to live in a safe, secure and home-like environment, and to move freely both within and outside the residential care service without undue restriction,
- be treated and accepted as an individual, and to have his or her individual preferences taken into account and treated with respect,
- continue his or her cultural and religious practices and to retain the language of his or her choice, without discrimination,
- select and maintain social and personal relationships with anyone else without fear, criticism or restriction,
- freedom of speech,
- maintain his or her personal independence,
- accept personal responsibility for his or her own actions and choices, even though some actions may involve an element of risk which the resident has the right to accept, and that should then not be used to prevent or restrict those actions,
- maintain control over, and to continue making decisions about, the personal aspects of his or her daily life, financial affairs and possessions,
- be involved in the activities, associations and friendships

of his or her choice, both within and outside the residential care service,
- have access to services and activities which are available generally in the community,
- be consulted on, and to choose to have input into, decisions about the living arrangements of the residential care service,
- have access to information about his or her rights, care, accommodation, and any other information which relates to him or her personally,
- complain and to take action to resolve disputes,
- have access to advocates and other avenues of redress, and
- be free from reprisal, or a well-founded fear of reprisal, in any form for taking action to enforce his or her rights.

Residents also have a responsibility to:

- respect the rights and needs of other people within the residential care service, and to respect the needs of the residential care service community as a whole,
- respect the rights of staff and the proprietor to work in an environment which is free from harassment,
- care for his or her own health and well-being as far as he or she is capable, and
- inform his or her medical practitioner, as far as he or she is able, about his or her relevant medical history and his or her current state of health.

(Copyright, Commonwealth of Australia; reproduced with permission.)

Government Regulations

Aged-care homes are regulated through a quality framework which includes certification (of the building and infrastructure) and accreditation (of the management, health care and residents' lifestyle).

Certification focuses on physical facilities and infrastructure of the home and is largely based on the Building Code of Australia. It includes regulations about safety, privacy, access, mobility, heating and cooling, lighting and ventilation and security. It is granted on the basis of continuous improvement via an agreed ten-year plan which provides the framework for improving safety, privacy and space standards.

Accreditation

The Australian Aged Care Quality Agency (**aacqa.gov.au**) is the independent organisation that administers the accreditation process on behalf of the Department of Health. The Agency conducts monitoring and assessment of homes as well as providing educational services and products to assist the industry improve its care for residents.

This quality process focuses on a home's policies and practices for delivering care for residents. There are four accreditation standards which derive from the *Aged Care Act 1997*:

- management systems, staffing and organisational development,
- health and personal care,
- resident lifestyle, and
- physical environment and safe systems.

There are forty-four expected outcomes from these four standards. These include continuous improvement, information systems, comments and complaints, medication management, pain management, palliative care, emotional support, privacy and dignity, leisure interests and activities, and cultural and spiritual life. Homes are required to maintain compliance with all expected outcomes at all times.

Homes are subject to a full audit at least every three years and will be subject to various in-between monitoring visits including at least one unannounced visit each year. The system is designed to encourage homes to continuously improve their practices while maintaining a resident focus.

Non-compliance

This occurs when a home is found not to be meeting one or more of the standards. When this is identified, the Agency may put the home on a timetable for improvement and this timetable will be monitored. If the home has not complied by the end of the timetable, then the Agency will conduct an audit (which may vary or revoke the home's accreditation) or recommend that sanctions be imposed. If the latter happens then details are posted on the Agency's website and on the myagedcare website's home-search page.

Prudential requirements

By 2010, over 63,000 bonds (now accommodation deposits) valued at over $10 billion were held in trust by homes all over Australia. All subsidised care-homes must comply with the prudential requirements that are defined in the *Aged Care*

(Bond Security) Amendment Bill 2013 (the Guarantee Scheme). If Mum's home becomes bankrupt or insolvent this scheme guarantees that any refundable lump sum balance will be repaid with interest. The government will then pursue the defaulting provider to recover this debt.

Chapter 8:
Finding a home

> **Information sources**
> 💻 **myagedcare.gov.au**
> ☎ **1800 200 422**

This is where the hard work starts but your first step should be to get a copy of the booklet *Five steps to entry in an aged care home* which is available from the myagedcare website in either printed form or you can download it. This will guide you through the process.

After that, you have two options — do it yourself or use a placement consultant. The do-it-yourself method is potentially cheaper (well, in terms of money but maybe not in terms of personal wear and tear) but may take longer. Using a placement service will have a direct financial cost attached to it but you will get the benefit of their local knowledge and up to date expertise of the whole system. But Mum will have to make a few decisions before you can embark on either path.

Mum's preferences

If Mum is still mentally alert, she will undoubtedly have views about her new environment, companions and the routine of her new home. A good place to start is to get her to make a list of her preferences but she also needs to understand that it might not be possible to supply them all. Once she has her list, get her to mark those must-haves as distinct from those things it would be nice to have. A few suggestions here to help her get started:

- geographic location,
- mentally alert companions,
- single room or shared, or a suite,
- bright and airy room with a nice view,
- extra services or not,
- multi-cultural environment or not, and
- specific activities inside or outside the home.

Geographic location

This is one of the first decisions that needs to be made. The big question could be 'your place or mine'. In other words, do you look for a home near where Mum is currently living (so her friends can visit easily) or do you move her close to you because you will still need to visit often. The choice may become more complicated if several family members or friends all want Mum to be near them — compromise will definitely be needed here.

If the choice involves an interstate move, then this choice may be tied up with your own family circumstances. This is not necessarily an easy decision and it is really important not to overlook or override Mum's wishes. If she is more than twenty minutes' drive away from her former home, then local friends will slowly but surely visit less frequently until they stop coming altogether.

> **Raymond's story**
>
> Raymond, a 91-year-old widower with no children, had advancing dementia but he was desperate to stay in his own home. After minor surgery he signed himself out of hospital in order to get home. His social worker told his niece that he needed to be in residential care and preferably in a distant town so that he couldn't just walk out to go home again.
>
> The niece organised a very nice room in a home that was thirty minutes' drive away. She lived hundreds of miles away and his local friends were of a similar age to Raymond and not big drivers. So it wasn't long before hardly anyone visited. He was isolate, lonely and became very depressed eventually declaring that, 'I *never* thought it would come to this.'
>
> **Lesson: Use a bit of common sense when working out the geographic preferences for Mum's home; the experts aren't always right.**

Mentally alert residents

A word here about mentally alert residents and those living with dementia. There have been two flow-on effects from the government's policy to support aged care in your own home:

- the average age of people moving into residential care has become older because they are staying at home longer, and
- the percentage of people living with dementia who are

moving into residential care for the first time, has also increased. In 2014 this figure was two-thirds of all new residents.

Alongside this, there is no longer any clear dividing line between low care and high care in residential homes. So if Mum's first choice of home intermixes residents (as 40% of homes do) then there is a chance that many of her neighbours in nearby rooms will be dementia residents. If she is still mentally alert then their unintended and unpredictable behaviour can become a real irritant — although homes must have mechanisms for managing these situations. It also has the potential to limit the number of new friends that she might make.

Lifelines

All of us have things in our lives that we couldn't do without and Mum will be no exception. One way to ease the transition is to ensure that she has these lifelines in place. For many the first one will be the phone — a lifeline to the outside world, family and friends. For the computer literate, it will be a computer with an internet connection, preferably in the quietness of her own room. If Mum is vision-impaired it might be audio books that keep her sane. If she is still actively involved in a hobby then this clearly will be important. Even though you might not have thought of them as lifelines before, now is the time to become aware of their significance and ensure they are high on the list of things to take.

Placement services

These are independent specialists who can find a home and arrange all aspects of a move. You can choose which and how many of their services you require. There is an Australia-wide list of these companies in the Resources in Part 4.

Their services are designed to provide practical assistance during all the steps of the placement process including:

- selection of a home,
- arranging visits,
- waiting list process,
- completion of admission stages,
- negotiation of the deposit,
- possibly financial advice through an allied financial adviser, and
- possibly providing support during the settling-in period

You and Mum will have to specify your location preferences, the type of home and room, her financial situation and any medical, cultural, religious or special requirements. You will also have to supply a copy of her ACAT approval. The consultant will research homes and provide you with a short-list so you can visit them before making that final choice.

Payment may be asked for as stage payments or an up-front deposit. Prices vary amongst agencies, but, as with most things in life, you get what you pay for. The benefits of using these services include:

- alleviating the stress of the process,
- you can be certain that all the important activities have been completed,

- it can be particularly useful if you need to find a home interstate. The consultants can do the legwork before you have to get on a plane to make that final choice.
- they will have considerable local knowledge of good and not-so-good homes that, as an outsider, you can't know,
- they will have good advice about what to look for and what to avoid, in your search and decision-making, and
- you may get greater added value when you need to pay an accommodation deposit because they can help negotiate this for you. They will be aware of how far each home can be pushed on this and they have prior experience of the process and protocols.

Yvonne's story

Yvonne was suddenly in the position of having to find a home, and fast, for her 98-year-old mother, who had been managing independently until unexpected surgery altered everything. Yvonne knew of several local homes and had half decided on one. But her own circumstances were such that she couldn't make the time to do all the legwork. Reluctantly (because of the cost) she approached a local agency.

The first thing they advised was not to use her chosen home ('nice people, but the quality of care could be better') and suggested an alternative. Yvonne expected that they would have to pay a bond, (Mum didn't have any assets — she had always rented her home), but the agency suggested that they could get her a place in an SRS home which meant no bond and good accommodation. Within the week Mum was settled in. And three years later she is still there and loving it.

Lesson: Don't assume and prejudge. If you don't ask, you don't get.

DIY search

This process is more or less one-step at a time. What we are describing from here on is the way to go providing you have the luxury of time. If you don't have this, then use the checklists in Part 4 to guide you through a fast-track version.

This is the wearing part for you, the carer. You will have to do all the visiting and assessing yourself. In an ideal world, there will be a number of homes in your chosen area, all with relatively short waiting lists, effectively giving you choice. In reality however, some areas have shortages of homes and others have longer lists, so your choices may be more restricted.

Make a short-list

To determine what level of care Mum is eligible to receive, she needs to have her ACAT assessment done (see Chapter 4) so you know what type of home and care you are seeking.

For up-to-date details of homes use the search facility at **myagedcare.gov.au/service-finder?tab=aged-care-homes**. Enter the suburb, click on permanent, and a list of homes in that area will come up on the next screen. Because the areas can be quite specific and sometimes small, you may have to repeat this using neighbouring suburbs or areas to find what you are looking for. You can copy and paste these details into a new Word document so you have a composite list at the end of your search.

If the resulting list looks daunting let's work out a strategy for managing this:

- Print off multiple copies of the list so that if you mess up the original, you still have spares.
- Decide a few criteria for visiting. Location is going to be one; any special requirements that Mum has identified will be another; ease of accessing them for visiting may be another so by grouping them, you may be able to visit several consecutively without driving miles in between. Have a look at the criteria in the checklists in Part 4 to see if anything else is important.
- Using these criteria, allocate priorities. Number the homes 1, 2, 3... in the order you would ideally like to visit them.

Background research

Before you start visiting, there are several internet-based sources of information where you can check your higher priority homes:

- the home's own website,
- myagedcare website by clicking on the home's name on the finder page,
- DPS *Guide to Aged Care*,
- independent ratings systems for homes, and
- Accreditation Agency's website.

The home's own website can provide much background information, like open days, times or days for inspections, facilities and any special services. A note of caution here. With both glossy leaflets and the internet (which is largely an electronic form of a printed brochure), you need to be alert to what they don't tell you. The pictures will be professional and smart and the residents will all look happy and content, but you won't get a feel for what the place is like at mealtimes or at midnight. The internet is a fabulous tool as long as you don't lose sight of its limitations.

There is also the DPS *Guide to Aged Care* which is available as a print book (one for each state or territory) or online at **agedcareguide.com.au.** This book only lists homes which advertise in it. Each listing shows an extensive range of details and it has helpful articles as well.

There are now two independent ratings systems for homes available at **agedcareonline.com.au/ratings** and **agedcarereportcard.com.au**. Any independent scheme like these is to be applauded for trying to provide an impartial view. However, these sites attempt to rate homes based a small number of criteria common to them all but you need to recognise that not all homes in Australia are participating in these schemes. Homes have to either register or advertise with the site and they are only going to do that when they can see a benefit. If Mum's preferred home suddenly shows up as 'the best home in South Australia' for instance, then it might only have been compared with a handful of other homes. So dig a bit deeper before you accept such a pronouncement.

The Australian Aged Care Quality Agency publishes the most recent publicly available report for every accredited home on its website at **aacqa.gov.au/site/pdfs/reports**. So read the home's most recent accreditation report for an accurate picture of the home. The Accreditation Agency's website also has a section with explanations for residents at **aacqa.gov.au/for-the-public**.

Tours

Before you start visiting homes, a word of advice about terminology.

Val's story

In the course of his work as an aged-care financial adviser, Val has visited many homes. He found that asking to do an 'inspection' was often received negatively but if he asked for a 'walk-through,' homes were often much more accommodating.

Lesson: Using positive language is always going to yield more beneficial results.

Each home has its own way of doing this. Smaller homes may take you round if you just turn up and ask. Others may want you to make an appointment which could be the same day. Larger homes are more likely to have specific days and times when they will take groups around or even have open days at a weekend. If the home's waiting list is particularly long, they may not be willing to show you round at all. However, if they have empty places which they are keen to fill, they may be more spontaneous and show you on the spot.

Anthea's story

One day I arrived unannounced at one large and well-regarded home explaining that I was looking for a home for my 90-something Mum. The receptionist gave me some leaflets but said that they weren't doing any tours at the moment because 'the waiting list isn't moving very fast!' In other words, they were looking after the residents so well that they were living longer so that the vacancy rate was slow.

Lesson: There are homes which are worth the wait.

If Mum is a bit frail or disabled, you may want to do a first round of visits to weed out those which aren't of interest. When you have a short-list, then this is the time to take her for a viewing.

If at all possible, it is really important that Mum sees the home — she is the person who will be living there. Visiting it is the only way that she can get a feel for the home and the people. If she is still mentally alert, she needs to be the one making this choice and decision. Put yourself in her shoes — how would you feel having your son or daughter telling you that this 'place', this building with its unknown environment, is going to be your home for the rest of your life?

In an ideal world, finding a home that Mum is happy with from the outset can avoid the heartache and stress of having to move her later on if she has become depressed because of her environment. But homes are also a changing environment. As some residents leave and new ones join, the mix of residents and the dynamics of their interactions will continually change, often with more people living with dementia moving in.

What to look for

There are criteria galore to consider when inspecting a home. However there are three acid tests and if any home fails any of these, cross it off your list without any further ado and move onto the next one. These are:

- is the exterior scruffy and unkempt?
- does it smell?
- what is your gut reaction?

Since you are unlikely to remember all the criteria that you need to consider, there is a comprehensive checklist in Part 4. If you are looking for a home with a secure dementia unit, there is an additional checklist of dementia-specific criteria to consider — use both lists.

If you are visiting several homes in one day, then photocopy the checklist so you have one for each home. Highlight your most important requirements before you leave home.

All that is left to do now is the hard yards. Ring and make an appointment. Make multiple copies of Mum's ACAT approval to show the homes — they need to be sure that they can provide the level of care that she needs. Take your lists, ACAT approval, a deep breath and your metaphoric stamina pills and go and visit them. Try not to visit too many in one day. Even with your lists you may get too confused and mentally exhausted to remember which home offered/did not offer what facilities.

Finally, if you like the home, don't forget to put Mum's name on the waiting list and then ask the three big questions…

- how long is the waiting list?
- can I have copy of your Resident's Agreement? and
- can I have a copy of your application form?

Activities

Of all the criteria shown on the checklists, it is worth talking about activities. These are not just to help the residents pass their days. They have a more serious underlying objective — avoiding depression. This is not meant to scare you but rather to make you alert to the reality that the incidence of depression in aged-care homes is higher than in the same age-group who live in the outside community.

The antidote to depression is activity. Not just any activity but those that genuinely appeal. Activities should include regular exercise groups and indoors activities which may or may not need staff involvement and outdoor events which might range from a walk in the park next door to a bus outing to the theatre or cinema or even lunch at a pub.

If you are seeking a home for Dad, then because men are in a minority in most homes, it is important to check that there are events or facilities which are suitable for him. Also check whether there are any activities in the evenings, particularly if Mum is a night owl and still mentally alert. These activities are more likely to be resident-run because there are fewer staff on duty in the evenings.

> **Michelle's story**
>
> During her search for a home for her widowed father Michelle came across an Eden Alternative home which had everything a still-active man could ask for: a number of other male residents, a small men's shed, a vegie garden that some of the men worked in and a snug decorated like a pub TV lounge for watching the football. She had viewed quite a number of homes before this and thought this was not only exceptional but exactly right for her father.
>
> **Lesson: Most homes will have facilities specifically for men, but occasionally you will find a gem.**

Resident's Agreement

Irrespective of which home Mum chooses, she or you will be expected to sign a Resident's Agreement when she moves in. If you particularly like a home when you visit, ask them for a copy of their Agreement so you can read it and potentially get legal advice about it well before moving-in day. Homes will not usually alter their standard agreement but they should be able to add in a special clause if Mum has a particular concern or you have negotiated a special deal.

It is a legally binding document that sets out the rights and obligations of both parties. Moving in establishes both a personal and a legal relationship between you or Mum and the management of the home. The Agreement should include details about:

- type of care and services provided,
- all financial details,
- house rules of the home,
- complaints procedures, and
- circumstances under which Mum could be asked to leave or change rooms.

Don't be rushed into signing it. You have twenty-eight days after moving in before legally, it must be signed.

After the visits

Immediately you leave the home, make notes on your checklist about your feelings and impressions. List the good and the not-so-good points. If you think of other things that you forgot to ask, go back and ask them while they are still fresh in your mind. When you get home, discuss it in detail with Mum. Try not to avoid her queries even if it means more work for you in the short-term.

Once you have discussed and absorbed it all, give it a rating from 1-10 where 1 is the worst and 10 is the best. Using your 1-10 ratings make a short-list of those which are your preferred options.

If Mum has been assessed for respite as well as permanent care, one strategy is to 'try before you buy'. This means getting her into this preferred home for respite — although a respite room may be less appealing (perhaps smaller or without a view) than rooms for permanent residents. Homes will often go out of their way to make Mum feel welcome and well looked after. They understand the emotional turmoil that she is going through and generally speaking will be empathic.

If she decides that she likes the lifestyle then you can take comfort in knowing that you aren't just dumping her. She has been able to decide for herself and has ownership of the final decision.

Applying to a home

Once you have your short-list of preferred homes, you need to put Mum's name on their waiting lists if you didn't do this when you visited. Each home will have its own application process and form. Hopefully, you have a copy of this from your visits but if not either email or phone to ask for one. It will ask for quite a lot of personal information as well as medical notes together with a copy of the ACAT approval.

Although this is not a legal requirement, many homes also ask for your personal financial information. You are not obliged to divulge any information at this stage and commercially speaking, it is better to keep the details to yourself.

If you are signing the form on Mum's behalf, you will also need to attach a copy of your authority, usually your Power of Attorney. Now you can send them off to your selected homes.

A home can only make you an offer when:

- it has a vacancy, and
- it can meet your care needs, and
- its business requirements enable it to make the offer.

Usually a home can only have a vacancy when a resident leaves so you are unlikely to get much notice before they make you an offer. They can't plan these things ahead but you and Mum need to have thought about it, in detail, beforehand so that when the offer comes you can accept fairly promptly. If you don't, there will be others in the queue who will.

You need to realise that homes may not make an offer on a first-come-first-served basis. They are likely to operate, at least in part, on a needs basis. This could mean that you might have had Mum's name down for twelve months and not heard from them but without you realising it, they have recognised that her needs are not pressing. If this happens then try getting in touch again when you feel that it is time that Mum moved in.

If you are keen on one particular home, use the squeaky-wheel principle and phone often to ask about availability. This way the home knows that they are your preferred home and that you have not accepted a place elsewhere.

Jean's story

At 92 Jean was finding it increasingly hard to manage at home alone. A friend took her to look at number of homes from which she finally selected her preferred choice. She put her name on the waiting lists of about five homes through this process.

As time passed Jean slowly became more dependent but she heard nothing from any of the homes. A year after her initial visit she made an appointment to have another look at her first choice and effectively jog their memory. This time she had the wit to take her walking frame to enhance the idea that she now needed more support. The admissions lady did acknowledge that yes it was now time, and within a month or so Jean had moved in.

Lesson: You need to understand the process from the home's perspective and not make assumptions about it.

If any of the homes you applied to, are part of a larger group which has homes in a number of areas, you may receive an offer from a distant home within the group. This can make visiting and supporting Mum logistically more difficult.

Only you can decide if this is practical, even on a short-term basis. If she needs a home as soon as possible, one option is to accept this offer now. If you then receive a later offer from another, closer home you can then decide whether or not to move her — bearing in mind the upheaval this will cause for everyone.

If Mum can't move in straight away, the home can hold the room for her for seven days but you will have to pay from the date you accept their offer.

Preparation at home

While you are out doing the hard yards, there are practical things that Mum can be doing at home. But it is equally important to take care of her emotional needs. This will be an ongoing issue for some time to come, if not for the rest of her life.

At this stage, she is facing a whole new life in an unknown home with an unknown routine and with new fellow residents and carers. In a nutshell, she is expected to start over at a time in her life when she is least capable, physically and emotionally, of adapting. She is likely to be scared at the prospect. Scared, upset, uncertain, lacking in confidence and just plain wobbly.

She may also be panicking about all the practical things that need to be done before she goes. If she has lived in her own home for many years there will be grief and loss, particularly if the house and her furniture have to be sold. She may also hope, realistically or not, that she will be able to return home someday.

Unfortunately, this is just another load for you, as her carer, to cope with. Try and be compassionate and understanding. Hold her hand and make her understand that you are not abandoning her. Don't lie to her — don't tell her she can come home again one day if you know that is highly unlikely. Explain as much as you can about the home's routine and the people.

One thing that may not become apparent to Mum until she gets there is that living in a care home can never be the same as living in her own home. In a care home she won't get one-to-one attention, as each staff member will have many residents to look after. If Mum has been used to you doing everything for her and almost on-demand, then you might want to try to get her to understand this difference before she moves.

Life in the home will also be lived around a set routine —

specific times for meals, getting up and going to bed. Many older people take comfort from such a routine but if Mum is not one of them, you will need to explain this to her too.

Things to take

Moving into residential care is a mini-version of moving house but in a way, this makes it all the harder. Because she will only be able to take a limited number of personal items, it can be difficult deciding what to take and what to leave behind. Chapter 7 gives details of what the homes will provide in the way of furniture and furnishings.

The first step might be for Mum to compile a utopian list of all those things that in an ideal world, she would like to have around her. Once you both know exactly what the chosen home will supply and what you need to bring, then you can whittle the list down if necessary. But the chances are that if you don't have specific items on the list in the first place, they will surely get overlooked in the stress of the actual move.

Mum doesn't need to make this list all at one sitting. Indeed, she is more likely to have a comprehensive list by adding to it over time as she remembers things. You can also suggest things for her to consider.

The other thing to realise is that this is not a once-only process. Other items can be taken in once she has moved. In fact, it may only be after she has settled into the new routine that she or you realises what these might be particularly if she still has access to her own home.

Sadie's story

After Sadie had been in her home for a few weeks she realised that a small fridge, kettle and mugs in her room would allow her to make herself and her visitors a cuppa at any time. So her family sorted this out for her.

She had also really missed not having her piano which was still in her own home. When the family asked the management, they were happy for it to be brought along. It was installed in a small lounge where the music wouldn't affect anyone else. As it turned out, there was an unexpected benefit. When Sadie was playing other residents would come and listen. On good days, they would even have a sing-a-long.

Lesson: If you don't ask, you don't get. Don't assume that it is out of the question.

Clothing

One thing that Mum can do in advance is decide what clothing she wants to take. Easy-to-launder clothes are recommended. Every item must be labelled with Mum's name (for identification in the laundry). Some homes will do this for you (at a cost) or you can order woven labels that you sew in or iron on (look on the internet for suppliers.) Do this well in advance as the labels can take time to arrive.

Pets

Many older folk will have pets which have provided companionship and a focus to their lives. So a move into a care home is likely to mean that Mum will have to be parted from her beloved pet. This in itself can be heart-breaking. Even if the pet goes to another family member who will care for it equally well, to Mum this can feel like a bereavement and the grieving may continue for months. This can be offset by bringing the pet in when you visit.

One answer to this is to find an Eden Alternative home — see Chapter 7 or their website at **edeninoznz.com.au**. This is an alternative model for running a care home which welcomes and encourages pets as an integral part of daily life.

Things to think about

On the day that Mum moves into the home, you and Mum are likely to be asked all manner of questions relating to her immediate and future needs right down to her wishes should she die. Some of these things need to be thought about and discussed beforehand:

- dietary needs,
- spiritual/religious/cultural needs and preferences,
- medication,
- extra treatments like a podiatrist or physio,
- doctor's details — if Mum's home is in a new area, you may need to find a new doctor for her or the home may have arrangements with their local clinic,
- primary contact for emergencies, as well as other contacts, and next-of-kin if this is a different person, and
- medical Power of Attorney.

Arguably the most important of these from the home's point of view, is the medical Power of Attorney. This defines Mum's wishes for medical treatment in the event that she cannot make or communicate them near the end of her life. From her point of view, it may be one of the more difficult things to decide, which is why having thought about it and set it up well in advance of moving, is practical preparation.

Chapter 9:
Moving in

Living in an aged-care home will mean that Mum spends most of her day with new people under the same roof, with limited personal space and in a more rigid and communal routine. If she was previously living alone then moving to a home is going to require a lot of adjustment, patience and tolerance.

One of the biggest adjustments can be socialising and getting used to communal dining with people who are initially strangers and maybe living with dementia. It also means getting used to someone else doing everyday chores like the laundry and cleaning, particularly as they are unlikely to do them in the same way that Mum used to. It will also entail living to a more rigid timetable — meals in particular, will be at set times, and the hairdresser for example, may only be available once or twice a week and visitors may only be allowed in at certain times.

However, moving to a home does not mean that Mum relinquishes control over the personal aspects of her daily life, her possessions or financial affairs. She also retains her rights as a citizen, her personal privacy, her right to have visitors, and to come and go as much as her health and abilities allow.

The days before the move

In an ideal situation, you will have access to Mum's room a day or two before she moves. This will enable you to bring her furniture in without having to work around her. Doing the following ahead of time will help:

- book a moving van,
- ask other family members or friends to help with the move,
- ring your phone supplier to arrange to have the phone connected, and
- complete and submit a postal redirection form at the Post Office (you will need your Power of Attorney to do this).

If you can also persuade some other family or friends to be early visitors in the first days or week, then this should help Mum to not feel so isolated or abandoned. She will be paying attention to how the family reacts to her new home.

Setting up the room

When you first walk into the room, it is likely to look and feel like an institution no matter how nice the home is. So that Mum can settle in more readily, it is important to set it up with her belongings right from the start so that her first sight of the room will at least be like a mini-version of her own home. The alternative is moving belongings in piecemeal over the coming days which can result in Mum staring at blank walls, wondering what on earth she has come to and desperately wanting to return home.

As you move her furniture in, make your best guess about

the optimal placements but remember that Mum might want things repositioned or when she has been there long enough she might prefer a different arrangement.

> **Anthea's story**
>
> I helped Athole's family find a home for her. The family moved her in and I visited several days later. I knocked on her door and went in. My heart instantly fell through my boots. Athole was in her chair in the far corner, with no pictures on the wall yet, no flowers, and hardly any of her own furniture. The feeling of 'institution' screamed at me. She looked so very lost and alone.
>
> This was no reflection on her family nor the home; the family had spent the previous seven months visiting Athole in one medical institution after another and were absolutely worn out. And although the home was a very nice one, my spontaneous reaction was, 'how awful' for her.
>
> **Lesson: Do soften the blow as much as you possibly can right from the beginning. Put yourself in Mum's shoes and think about how you would feel in her situation.**

Phone

Assuming that Mum wants to have a landline phone in her room (she will still be responsible for the phone bills) then arranging this ahead of her move will mean that the delay between ordering and the connection actually happening, should be minimal. Telstra should not have to visit her room to do this installation. Occasionally there can be a delay because the previous occupant or their family has not disconnected their phone, so that technically this line is not available. If this should happen then ask the home to contact the family for you.

An alternative to a landline is to buy a simple mobile phone — or Mum might want both. If she chooses to leave the home later on, you do not incur the costs of installing and disconnecting the landline phone and you avoid the monthly line rental.

Although this is not an endorsement, there are two brands of mobile phones specifically designed for elderly or disabled folk who may not have had much experience with such devices. Ownfone and KISA Phone both have models with limited menus based on names not keypads on the front of the device (see their websites).

Pre-paid mobiles are not necessarily easier. Mum may use up all her credit without realising just how long she can talk without it running out. Then she might be reluctant to use it because she is now aware of the costs. You may also have to show her how to use it, possibly several times.

Moving-in day

This is likely to be one of the most stressful days in the whole process. To make the day run as smoothly as possible, let's start by looking at your objectives They are likely to be to:

- move Mum in safely and with a minimum of physical disruption,
- get her settled in as comfortably as possible and with the least amount of emotional upset, and
- minimise the emotional upheaval for everyone else.

Everything you do should be around these three goals and one of the best ways to meet these is to set up her room a day or two prior to her arrival if you can.

Let's say you have just received the phone call from your preferred home, offering Mum a place and that you accept. The first thing to realise is that you don't have to move instantly. You will have time to move over the next few days but if the call has come late in the afternoon, then this is clearly not a sensible thing to be doing right away. But be aware that you will have to pay the fees from the date you agree to become a resident.

If Mum is moving from hospital or transition care then her transport is likely to be arranged by the social worker. Her personal belongs will be packed and her move will be direct and efficient.

Things to take with you

The first thing to realise is that you don't have to take everything with you on the first day. You can add — and remove — things as Mum adjusts to her new life style. You will obviously need to take Mum's clothing (already labelled), her wash bag and whatever personal items she wants with her. Also, take at least one vase, her radio, television (if it's not provided) and a clock that she can see. For her health care, you should also take:

- all her medications and prescriptions,
- her glasses and a spare pair if possible,
- her hearing aids and a spare pair of these as well, and
- any other aids.

You will also need to take some paperwork with you, in particular:

- her Powers of Attorney,
- her Medicare card,
- her ambulance insurance/card,
- her private health insurance details, and
- the Resident's Agreement if you previously were given a copy.

On arrival

The preferred time for everyone, staff and family, is to arrive during the day. There are always more staff on during day shifts, including a receptionist or admissions person who will help with the admission paperwork. Whether it is morning or afternoon is really up to you, as long as the home knows more or less when to expect you.

The admission paperwork can take between half to one hour, depending on its complexity. If you have done the preparation we talked about in Chapter 8, then it should be easier.

The home will expect you or Mum to sign the Resident's Agreement today. However it should only be signed once you or she is happy with its contents and she understands it. This is particularly true for the fees and charges clauses which should have been agreed before she moves in. If Mum is physically unable to sign but can understand it and is willing to sign, she can ask a person with a Power of Attorney to sign on her behalf. Once she has signed it and moved in, her place is secure.

Settling Mum in

Once she is installed, chatting about what she wants put where can be a practical distraction. Bringing her own bed covers is a big step towards personalising the room. Photos will also make all the difference, as will pictures on the walls although the home may stipulate that their staff actually hang the pictures. Getting some fresh flowers or a pot plant from day one, will remind Mum of you once you have left for the day and help reduce her loneliness.

It is probably inevitable that things have been left behind or forgotten in the move, so remember to take a pen and paper so you can make a list. If Mum is able, taking her to the shops or back home to get some of these items can also be a distraction, even in the days to come. In the longer run it may well turn out that she does not feel the need to go back to her old home.

This may be the first time Mum has been inside the home. Even if it isn't, the following suggestions can help her get oriented and settled:

- make sure that the call button works and is within easy reach,
- make sure that her radio (and TV) are plugged in and work; that the remote controls work and are within easy reach,
- adjust the room temperature to suit the day and time of year,
- explain when the next meal time is and how the dining room process works,
- explain how the bathroom works particularly the shower controls,

- point out where the light switches are including the nightlight if there is one, and
- take Mum on a tour of the home.

Stay with Mum as long as you feel it is appropriate. When the next meal time arrives, you can go with her to the dining room — if you have planned ahead and booked a meal, you could eat with her too. This is a good time to introduce Mum and yourself to the others at her table or nearby. Also, introduce her to the dining-room staff if they don't already know to expect her.

Risk of loss

Loss of property is going to be an ongoing concern, particularly if confused or dementia residents are within Mum's vicinity. People living with dementia sometimes wander and take things just because they are on show without understanding what they are doing. Do not leave cash, bank or credit cards, cheque books or valuables in Mum's room, not even if they are locked away. Mum is likely to want to keep wearing her rings so you need to keep a wary eye in the future to be sure that these haven't disappeared. It can be a good idea to take photos of them when she first moves in.

Leaving

This could be the hardest part of the day for everyone so a few strategies to help here:

- tell Mum when you will next be able to visit,
- also tell her if someone else is going to visit first,

- be totally honest with her — don't make false promises or set up false expectations, and
- there are bound to be tears or signs of upset. Try to respond with understanding and don't be patronising or dismissive.

This could also be the point at which you come apart. Hopefully, you will have support from the others who have helped you during the day. If it is now evening, then going out for dinner with them will be one way of talking it out of your system and bringing closure to the day.

Chapter 10:
The first weeks

Mum is going to take quite some time to adjust to her new surroundings and routine. At least a month, possibly several. She has been completely removed from her comfort zone and her own routine in the space of just one day. She is likely to be feeling grief and loss (of her independence, her home and possessions, her pets) and abandonment.

If Mum has come from her own home even if this was a small apartment, moving to live her whole life in a single room is likely to feel extremely restrictive to the point of being claustrophobic. Try to encourage her to use the home's facilities, the lounge and outdoor spaces as well as taking part in their activities.

She may also be confused by the geography of her new surroundings, and feel overwhelmed that she has to make friends with all these unknown fellow residents. The dementia residents will have unpredictable and unusual behaviour which is a whole new lifestyle issue and potential irritant she has to learn to cope with.

The care home should understand Mum's mixed emotions and take steps to help her settle in. However it is always a good idea to ask them how Mum is doing and if there is anything that you, her main carer, can do to help.

If Mum is in the home because the family has recognised the

need for this move, but she does not see it or perhaps does not agree, then she is likely to also be resentful, frustrated or just plain angry. She may feel trapped in a situation from which she sees no escape. Over the coming weeks take her home for the weekend and let her try to manage on her own. The chances are she will not cope as well as she imagined and in time she will come to realise the benefits of the move. As one carer commented, 'It's the agony and the ecstasy. The agony of leaving your own home but the ecstasy of never having to cook or clean again.'

As the main carer, you too will have a period of adjustment to cope with. Initially take time out to recover, to recharge your batteries and indulge in a little pampering — you deserve it. Be sensitive to Mum's situation through this time — she may react or behave differently each time you visit. This doesn't necessarily mean there is a big problem or that she is reacting against you; it could just be part of her own settling-in process.

How the home operates

Now that Mum is safely tucked up in a home, don't think that, apart from the occasional visit that is the end of it. In many ways that was only the end of phase one with phase two, the ongoing support, just beginning. The first thing to do for both of you really is learn how the home works in detail. Just a few things to think about:

- the main meal of the day may be at lunch time,
- can Mum book visitors in to have a meal with her? If so is there a cost?
- the dining room arrangements are likely to be permanent

so that Mum eats with the same people each time. Mum should be able to ask to change tables if she wants to sit with someone else,
- how often does the laundry get collected and delivered?
- when is the mail delivered and does the home open it first?
- is there a room which can be booked for private meetings or functions?
- Mum must sign out when she leaves the building for an outing and she must sign back in when she returns,
- all visitors must sign in and out when they visit — this a fire precaution,
- if Mum is still driving she should be able to take her car to the home,
- can the staff come into Mum's room at night? If she doesn't want or need this then ask the staff to put a notice on her door,
- if Mum has previously set up enduring doctor's referrals for regular specialist appointments and she has had to change to a new GP when she moved in, she will have to ask for replacement referrals,
- when Mum gets her bill from the visiting GP, it is probable that the Medicare rebate has not been applied and you will have to do this separately. This also applies to any services like physio that she wants to claim on her health insurance, and
- arrange to have her medical history sent to the new doctor if her own doctor cannot continue.

Things the home will do

Apart from the staff getting to know Mum and vice-versa, there are several processes that the home will do which may not be apparent to either of you. The main ones are setting up a care plan and asking her to complete an advanced care directive.

Care plan

This is the document which will spell out Mum's medical and ancillary needs. On admission, the nursing staff will set up a general plan so that things like Mum's medication all happen when they need to.

Over the following weeks, they will make it more detailed as they observe her and talk to her GP, physio and any other allied staff. As you have been Mum's main or only carer for months now, you know her likes and dislikes as well as her needs. Your insights should be an important input into the plan. Over time, the plan will be reviewed both periodically and in response to any changes in her condition. Provided you are Mum's Power of Attorney, you can ask to see it at any time.

If you have a major concern, then talk to the DON first. Also check in the Resident's Agreement for any rules about this sort of situation. If you aren't happy with the DON's response then a complaints procedure will be given in the Resident's Agreement.

Advanced care directive

This is a document which all homes are required to set in place fairly soon after Mum arrives. It is likely to be a form asking lots of questions about her wishes as she approaches death.

This will include details of your preferred funeral director, any personal wants like clothing or music and who and when the home should ring. Mum might find this process a bit daunting or upsetting in which case leave it till your next visit.

Things you can do

There are still plenty of loose ends to be tied up some of which will require you to use your Power of Attorney.

Change of address

Apart from family and friends all these organisations need to be notified of Mum's new address and some of them will be straightforward; others will be bureaucratic and hard work.

- her doctor and any specialists,
- her community nurse or community care provider,
- meals-on-wheels and any other support services she has been using,
- her private health insurance company,
- her superannuation company,
- her solicitor, accountant and financial adviser, stock broker,
- the roads authority (for her driver's licence),
- her bank, building society or credit union,
- other aged-care homes you applied to,
- Medicare,
- Centrelink and/or the DVA,
- Australian Taxation Office,

- Australia Post for redirection of her mail (if you haven't done it earlier),
- Australian Electoral Commission (for the electoral roll), and
- utility companies and the local council if she still has a family or holiday home.

Photo ID

One really bureaucratic process arises in relation to photo ID. If Mum has given up her driving licence and therefore has no form of ID but still needs this, say for use at her bank then there are two options open to you. The Keypass card is a national photo ID card available through the Post Office or a Proof of Age card which is a state-issued card and is available online. Both cards will require that she has an up to date photo which may entail a trip to the Post Office. The Keypass application needs to see the usual hundred points of identification which by definition is almost impossible if Mum no longer has her licence or a passport and has sold her house. It is possible to work your way through this system but you may well need fortitude and stamina.

Financial affairs

If Mum is a Centrelink or DVA pensioner and she has made changes to her financial circumstances (such as paying a deposit to the home), you should notify Centrelink or the DVA of these changes (if you haven't already done this) so they can update her income and asset details.

Arrangements can be made with Centrelink to appoint a correspondence nominee. This is someone who Mum has nominated to receive copies of all correspondence that Centrelink would otherwise have sent to her. The nominee then can assume responsibility for taking whatever action is required.

The level of complexity of Mum's financial affairs will determine the best approach to managing them. If they are relatively straightforward then she might decide to keep managing everything herself.

If her affairs are more complex and she doesn't want to keep doing it herself, then her next alternative would be to ask a family member to do it for her. She would need to sign a Power of Attorney to empower this person to act on her behalf. If this is not appropriate or possible, then she should consult a professional adviser (accountant, solicitor or financial adviser) who is willing to pay all her expenses, receive and bank all her income and provide regular financial reports to her and the family.

Mum's financial correspondence will also need to be filed and her bank records monitored to make sure that her income and cash availability continues to be sufficient for her needs. There should also be a back-up plan in case she suddenly wants access to large sums for whatever reason, or if her income doesn't quite cover her expenses.

Residents who have little or no family and need to set up a Power of Attorney have been known to ask other professionals to act on their behalf. Whilst accountants are able to do this, other providers like placement services or staff at the home cannot do this or enter into any other legal relationship on her behalf. Not only would it be unprofessional on their part, but it would also set up a conflict of interest. Sometimes this can be resolved simply by appointing an additional signatory on her cheque account or setting up direct debits on her account.

Care home fees and pharmacy bills should be monitored regularly. Pharmacy costs are quite often complex and mistakes can occur including over-supply, and therefore over-charging, of medications.

If Mum's financial circumstances change significantly then this may be an opportunity for a financial reassessment by Centrelink. If you take over her affairs at some point because she can no longer cope herself, then review her fees and get financial advice if you are concerned.

Chapter 11:
Ongoing practical issues

> 🖥 **myagedcare.gov.au**
> ☎ 1800 200 422
> Complaints ☎ 1800 200 422
> Advocacy ☎ 1800 700 600

There are many things that you can do either to improve Mum's lot or to ensure that she is being looked after satisfactorily. You may notice that certain aspects of the home aren't quite as good or to Mum's liking as you'd hoped, maybe the food or activities. This may entail you coming up with alternatives to supplement or replace what is on offer, or making requests or giving feedback to staff to get things changed. Homes are expected to make continuing improvements so your comments can become one source for this.

As time passes and Mum deteriorates, it may be that you will need to visit more often or keep a watchful eye out for her care and health. You may have to be more proactive and critical. As she settles in, she may want other items in her room and possibly not need some of the original things she brought with her.

Your relationship with her may change. Many of the tasks you previously did are no longer your responsibility. The amount of time you spend with her and the nature of your interactions are going to be different. But just because Mum is in a home, this is no reason for treating her with any less respect and dignity. So a few tips to help you maintain these qualities for her:

- when you are talking to her, sit or squat at her level, so your eyes make direct contact and you don't appear to be dominating, talking down or patronising her,
- preserving her independence as much as possible also preserves her self-respect. Only offer to help when it is asked for and never insist on doing something for her.
- make sure she always has some cash in her purse. This helps to retain her independence and feel like an adult, and
- keep an eye and ear open to ensure that the staff also treat her with respect and dignity.

Some of the following suggestions may be obvious, but other suggestions have come from aged-care nurses who speak from their many collective years of experience.

Conversations

As time passes and you get on with your own life, it is easy to feel that you have no common ground with Mum any more. Her life is now constrained to the four walls of her room, the staff and fellow residents of the home and her interests are tightly focused around her daily routine. The following suggestions might help in this regard.

If Mum suffers from memory loss or dementia, buy a nice

exercise book or journal and leave it in her room to be used as a communication book. Encourage everyone who visits to write in it. Photos and other memorabilia can be added to show her on her good days. But more importantly the staff can write any messages for you in the book as well. This way you will receive the message when she is unlikely to remember to tell you.

If you take some flowers or chocolates, this can become the basis for conversation. It also tells Mum that she is still special.

Learn to listen, really listen — let Mum talk, don't interrupt her, nod occasionally to acknowledge you are listening, ask questions or for more details.

Don't ask yes/no questions. You can't make a conversation any shorter than by seeking single syllable answers. Ask open questions, (how, what, where, when, why questions). This will encourage Mum to tell you what's been going on (or not as the case may be), what she might want/need or any problems that she might be having.

There is something called Validation Theory that works wonderfully for folk whose mental faculties aren't quite on the same plane as yours. If Mum starts to waffle or you have no idea what she is on about, don't argue or debate it with her; just agree. Simple stuff. But it can also be her way of telling you something important.

Cynthia's story

Cynthia, an aged-care nurse, overhead this conversation between a daughter and her bed-bound Mum. Mum suddenly commented on the big hole in the ceiling and how the rain dripped all over her last night. The daughter instinctively looked at the ceiling which was obviously intact. But she asked Mum, 'Where did the rain make you wet?' Mum vaguely pointed to the bed. When Cynthia peeled back the covers, what did she find but a wet bed!

Lesson: Don't dismiss Mum's ramblings as meaningless — this may be the only way she can now communicate.

Mental stimulus

If Mum is still mentally alert, she is going to need this — without it she runs the risk of falling into depression so here are some ideas about how to help maintain this.

Have a conversation about current affairs or some other topical subject. Because they have time on their hands, older folk often listen regularly to the radio or watch the news. As a result, they can be very up-to-date with all sorts of things but they may have no one with whom they can discuss them.

Take her out for a drive or to visit friends. Take her shopping or to the cinema or other local activities including church if she is a churchgoer. Help her maintain any previous contacts or social activities. Take her out for a meal or coffee.

Ensure that her TV and radio are accessible so she can turn them on or off (or has easy access to the remote control). Are they tuned in correctly? Mum won't always want to sit in the communal lounge to watch TV.

Take books and/or magazines.

If her vision is impaired, or perhaps English is not her first language and reading is difficult, tune the radio into Vision Australia Radio (which broadcasts for the print handicapped on various FM frequencies in Victoria and southern NSW). For details see **radio.visionaustralia.org/**

Take in audio books (which can be borrowed from the local library) or join Vision Australia's library for free and regular deliveries for the vision impaired. Details at **visionaustralia. org/living-with-low-vision/library.** Audio books can also be purchased from Amazon and played on tablets or smart phones.

Pam's story

Mum was 97, still fully mentally alert and capable of intelligent conversation but her increasingly frail physical condition resulted in her moving into a home in a high-care unit.

What Pam hadn't appreciated was that the majority of high-care residents have some degree of dementia making intelligent conversation almost impossible. Although Mum had her mental needs met to some extent through the radio and books, it was less than a week before she was frustrated, angry and demanding that Pam, 'get her out of this place'.

Lesson: No amount of activities can replace the stimulus from human interaction.

Activities

These are going to be a fundamental part of keeping Mum focused and giving her a reason for getting out of bed in the morning. Chapters 8 and 11 both talk about the importance of activities as a means of avoiding depression.

Firstly, you would hope that the home you have chosen offers activities that are of interest. It may also be that Mum has taken her own activities with her, things like crosswords, jigsaw puzzles, knitting or books. Keeping her own interests going obviously does not preclude her from joining in the communal activities of her choice. And the communal program is one means of avoiding the isolation that can arise, particularly if she spends a lot of time in her room.

External activities are almost more important if this is still practical. This might include shopping, visiting friends or family, going out for lunch or taking Mum to church or church-based events. These serve to connect (or reconnect) her with the wider world giving her more to talk about and make her feel she is not completely in God's waiting room. If the home has a community bus then taking part in the offered outings will help keep her connected with the outside world.

Mum may be able to adapt her interests. In her younger days, she may have been a skilled musician. Now that her eyesight is not so good, reading the music is more difficult. Hopefully she can adapt to play less demanding pieces.

Physical exercise is something that is just as important at this stage in life as it is at any other. The home should run regular exercise groups where the activities are modified to a level that fits the capabilities of the residents. These are fundamental for maintaining a healthy physical, mental and emotional lifestyle. Even a gentle walk around the grounds is fine and if Mum only does this on her good days, then that is still better than not at all.

If there are no scheduled activities in the evenings, ask the Lifestyle Manager if something can be arranged. Screening movies from DVDs are particularly easy and require very little staff involvement. If Mum is still alert and physically able, she could offer her services to organise or run this, or perhaps a bingo session.

Jean's story

It didn't take Jean long to be chomping at the bit because there were no evening activities in her new home. The Lifestyle Manager explained that things like scrabble or jigsaws didn't work because the residents with dementia tended to take pieces so you could never complete the game. Jean asked about movies saying she was perfectly willing to switch the player on and off each time. The home scheduled evening movies several times a week, supplied the DVD and left Jean to run it. A win-win.

Lesson: The home needs the feedback and welcomes the residents' active involvement.

Practicalities

If Mum is on a lot of different medications and she has brought both the prescriptions and her current stock of pills with her, then the DON or the nurse in charge will want to take over responsibility for them immediately. It is helpful if you understand their procedure for reordering. If Mum has had to accept a new doctor then it may be that the home won't accept her existing scripts or supplies. This can result in Mum having to pay again for medication that she already had when she moved in.

Helena's story

Helena had glaucoma amongst many other things and when she moved into her up-market home, she took her stock of six months of prescription eye drops. Unbeknownst to her, the home's routine for drug ordering was to have the chemist deliver residents' ongoing medication at the start of each month. Helena moved in at the end of one month, and within a week she had a chemist's bill for the same eye drops.

Lesson: Ask and make sure you understand the home's routine for ordering medicines, but also be firm about ensuring they accept that Mum's existing supplies are valid and usable.

Some more practical things:

Visit fairly often — or spread the visits across a number of family members and friends. While this obviously brings pleasure and a focus to Mum's day, what is less obvious is that the staff may be more careful about how they treat Mum because they know the family are frequent visitors and alert to unexpected changes.

Visit at meal times — your reaction to this may be that you would be interrupting their routine, but this is a good opportunity to check out the quality of the food, what the portion sizes are like and if any special dietary needs are being met. Even better, book in to have lunch or dinner at the home with Mum so that, most important of all, you can check that she is still eating and has not lost her appetite.

Neil's story

Neil visited his Mum one day at lunchtime — the main meal of the day — only to learn that her food was always cold when it arrived. It turned out that she was the last one to be served.

He mentioned this to the staff and they altered the order in which they served the residents. Problem solved. But had he not visited at lunchtime, this minor but irritating issue would not have been discovered.

Lesson: Just because Mum mightn't mention a problem, doesn't always mean there isn't one. Use your own eyes and ears to ensure her well-being.

Talk to the staff — the first time you do this, ask who is the most appropriate person to talk to. If they do not wear uniforms you could be talking to the cleaner without realising it. If they do wear uniforms, do you understand the different styles? Ask for a person's name and title because on your next visit you might need to speak to her/his colleague on another shift. (See Chapter 7 for details of who's who in a home.) The ideal staff-family relationship should be collaborative, co-operative and realistic.

Do volunteer work for the home — they will be more alert to Mum's needs as a result. But be aware that volunteers are now required to pass a police check if they have direct contact with residents.

Occasionally take a gift for the staff. If you only do this at Christmas, yours might be indistinguishable from all the rest they receive at this time. Do it when it can make a bigger impact which may also have a beneficial spin-off for Mum. When she goes on outings she can also bring small gifts back for her favourite staff members.

When you go on holidays send her postcards and pictures. If she can use a computer then emails with pictures attached or posting them on Facebook are more immediate ways of making her still feel part of the family.

You will need to work out a way for Mum to be able to top up her supplies of cash. Taking her to the bank makes an outing of it; otherwise you might have to do this regularly for her.

Give Mum a focus and something to look forward to every day.

> **Bryan's story**
>
> After some weeks in her home, Bryan's Mum was losing interest in her surroundings. The DON asked Bryan what they could do to reconnect her to her former life. 'A small glass of sherry before dinner would help enormously', was the reply. And indeed it did — it gave her something to look forward to each day.
>
> **Lesson: Even if the lifeline is outside the home's rules or norm, still ask.**

Although the home's laundry is fine for everyday clothing, if Mum has any special belongings, like a mohair rug or a silk blouse, then take these home and launder them yourself. They are likely to survive better with personal handling. You might also find that items go missing regardless of how well labelled they are. Mention it to the person in charge.

Check on small valuable items like jewellery. Make sure that Mum's rings haven't suddenly disappeared and when you ask, they have accidentally 'fallen down the drain/toilet'.

Befriend the maintenance staff — there will be times when Mum needs a light globe changed or other small things fixed or altered. If you can ask this person directly you avoid any bureaucracy and the matter will very likely get attended to faster.

If Mum appears to becoming depressed or disinterested, encourage her to take part in some of the activities on offer or ask if there are any outside activities that she would like to get involved in. It is obviously better if you can prevent this, by having her join in early on.

When Mum's birthday comes around, the home is likely to

commemorate this day with a birthday cake, maybe at afternoon tea time in the lounge. It might even be a special one like 80 or 90 years. Like any other birthday, these warrant a celebration. If you can take her out then so much the better. You or she can choose how you will celebrate. If she can't get out, then you will have to bring the celebration to her — with the home's help and agreement of course.

Neil's story

Neil's Mum turned 80 while she was living in her care home and Neil decided to have a party. With the home's agreement, they used a courtyard and an adjoining room. They planned their menu of cold finger food to make it easy.

On the day they used the room to serve the food and drinks and collect up the dirty dishes. They invited all Mum's friends and family who met up in the warm sunny courtyard. And Mum's crowning joy was the special cake and having all her important people with her to share her day.

Lesson: Make the most of every remaining day. You just don't know how many there will be.

One-off possibilities

There will be any number of practical issues that will arise over the weeks and months as both you and Mum get used to the new environment and how it works. But there are a few bigger situations that could arise although the following list is by no means exhaustive.

If Mum feels lonely or isolated, the Community Visitors Scheme (CVS) may be a solution. This is a government-funded scheme which provides one-on-one volunteer visitors to residents who would benefit from the companionship. If she or you feel there is such a need, then advise the person in charge. They will get in touch with the CVS which will take into account Mum's interests, hobbies and background in trying to match her with a suitable companion. The scheme is available to anyone living in a home that receives a government subsidy and who is identified as being at risk of isolation or loneliness.

If Mum would like a few days away staying with family or even a longer holiday, she can be away for up to fifty-two nights in a financial year. She will have to pay her usual fees (and the government continues with its subsidies) during any absence. This is called social leave and only counts if she is away overnight. If she is away for more than fifty-two nights, the government will not pay the subsidies and you may be asked to make up the difference.

If Mum has to go into hospital for any reason the home will keep her room for her but she will still have to pay the fees. This is not counted as social leave.

For whatever reason, Mum may decide that she would like to change rooms. You need to lodge the request with the manager and all such requests must be considered even if it isn't possible to move her immediately. You should also check the Resident's Agreement for any rules about this.

The home could ask Mum to move rooms if there are repairs or improvements to be made to her room, or if it has been upgraded to extra services and you don't want to pay the additional fees. Either way Mum must be fully consulted and agree without being pressured.

Residents and Relatives Groups

Most homes will have a regular forum called a Residents and Relatives Group (or something similar) which is a vehicle for everyone (staff, residents and families) to raise issues about the home. Meetings are usually quarterly.

The DON and/or the Manager may wish to tell everyone about new ideas or changes in the home that are coming up and this is the ideal forum. Similarly, residents or relatives may have issues or ideas for improvements that would benefit from a communal discussion. If Mum is fairly new in the home and you are having problems, other members of the group who have been involved for much longer, can be helpful in explaining the inner workings or providing suggestions for solving a particular issue.

Joining this group will keep you up to date with what's going on in the home, help you to meet other people who are in a similar situation to yourself and will make the staff aware that you are looking out for Mum's welfare.

Outside the home

Even though Mum is now living in a home, she still has relationships with outside organisations including her bank, Centrelink/DVA and the tax office. If she still owns her house, then there are all the organisations and services associated with that. All these need to be maintained either by you or by her.

On the day she moved in, and possibly since, Mum will have taken what clothes she wants with her. As she adapts to the new lifestyle, it will become apparent that many of the clothes she has left behind are now redundant. As part of her own process of coming to terms with living in a care home, she needs to decide how these are to be disposed of. You could try bringing them into the home, maybe in small lots, so she can decide for herself. Alternatively you could take her back home to work through this. This is likely to also be true for other personal possessions.

Moving

To another home

In the early days or months, Mum may receive an offer from an alternative home that you applied to at the outset. She is at liberty to move to a new home at any stage but to be safe, check the details in the Resident's Agreement before you start the process.

It may be that her home changes ownership and as a result, the procedures, food or other things change in such a way that is not to Mum's liking. Or eventually you or she may decide to move elsewhere for a number of reasons.

If you are concerned that this move may not altogether be necessary, then you should discuss it with the DON and/or the manager to start with. If you are still not convinced then ask Mum's GP for their suggestions. But throughout, try not to lose sight of what is in her best interest. It might be better to stay rather than face the disruption and the resettling process that a move would entail.

If you do start this process, it is really important to take her to visit the new home. By this time she has gained considerable experience and insight into the way a home works — and doesn't work. She will also have refined her list of needs and priorities.

Anita's story

Anita's husband David suffered from a progressively degenerative disease. They moved from their family home to a retirement village as his condition worsened. As he became increasingly debilitated, it was obvious that he needed nursing care and he was subsequently assessed as residential high care.

Anita searched and found several homes that would suit but none had an immediate vacancy. Out of necessity, she accepted the first offer, a less-than-perfect choice as he had to share a room on the first floor in a fairly clinical environment. Anita left his name on the other waiting lists. A smaller home much closer offered Anita a single room on the ground floor. Needless to say, she accepted.

The family moved David within the week and the move was, in Anita's words, 'seamless'. A rare accolade. The result is a win-win. David is more comfortable, he is getting better care (because it is smaller), and he has easy access to the garden. Anita's stress is lessened because the care is better and the home is much closer for her daily visits.

Lesson: Moving to another home is not necessarily a nightmare. You now have prior experience to ease the process and understand what other resources are available.

To hospital

If Mum has had an accident or an illness which has resulted in an unexpected stay in hospital or her condition is continuing to deteriorate, then her current home may not be keen for her to return because she now needs a level of care that they cannot provide. These situations can arise at short notice so you may not be prepared for the need to take immediate action.

You may also disagree with the home. Under these conditions, there are several things you can do:

- firstly check the Resident's Agreement to see exactly what your position is if only for the interim and to give yourself time to find an alternative.
- discuss it with the home and Mum's doctor.
- the hospital will understandably want Mum out as soon as possible and should advise you if there are any local transition care facilities.
- contact Elders Rights Advocacy (see Resources in Part 4) for advice, support, and if necessary, advocacy.

To transition care

Transition care is an interim step in the aged-care system which provides a short-term care solution. Hospitals will want Mum to vacate her bed as soon as possible and if you haven't found a new home for her, then she could go to transition care for up to twelve weeks, providing there is one locally and they have a vacancy. This gives you time to find a permanent solution. It also creates an opportunity for Mum to get physically stronger before the move because transition care provides low-intensity therapies (such as physio or occupational therapy) and support as part of an ongoing recovery process.

To specialised care

There may come a time when Mum starts behaving in an irrational or challenging manner. This can include wandering, aggression or screaming. The home may reasonably feel that providing this level of care is beyond its capabilities and specialised care is needed. The two most common forms are dementia care and psycho-geriatric care homes — see Chapter 13.

Mum is asked to move

There are a number of legitimate reasons why a home might ask Mum to leave:

- the home is closing,
- there are disruptive repairs or improvements to be done to the home,
- the home changes to extra services and you choose not to pay the additional costs,
- the home can no longer provide the care that Mum needs,
- she no longer needs the care provided by the home,
- she has not paid an agreed fee within forty-two days after the due date for a reason within your control, or
- she has intentionally caused serious damage to the home or serious injury to a member of staff or to another resident.

If Mum is asked to move, the reason should be one that

is specified in her Resident's Agreement. She must be fully consulted and agree without being pressured. The home should help you find alternative accommodation that meets her assessed long-term needs and is affordable. She should also be given notice, in writing, fourteen days before she needs to leave.

Complaints

In her early days, in particular when she is still adjusting to the home's routine, Mum might find any number of little things irritating. Some might be for reasons that are not immediately obvious to a newcomer, but others might just as easily be rectified with a word in the right ear. Sometimes solutions can be simple like a notice on her door asking visitors to please close the door.

However, despite your best efforts with both Mum and the home, occasionally it becomes necessary to raise a concern that may escalate into a complaint. If it is something minor that can be resolved by making a request or suggestion to the staff then this is by far the best way to resolve the issue.

If however, this doesn't sort out the problem, then every home is required to have a formal process for handling complaints and details will be in the Resident's Agreement. If you don't have them, then you should ask for a copy. Additionally you can check on the notice board for any information or ask at your Residents and Relatives Group for advice.

The home should help you through this process. It can become a daunting prospect so try to have some additional support like a family member or friend with you when you raise the issue.

Many homes see complaints as a way to make improvements so they can also have a beneficial flow-on effect for everyone.

If the situation doesn't get resolved internally or you feel that the issue is too great to be handled in this way, there are external authorities which can help. However, you need to be aware that this process can be both time-consuming and stressful. There are two programs which are available:

- Aged Care Complaints on **1800 200 422** is a free service which investigates concerns about the health, safety or well-being of people receiving aged care. See also **agedcarecomplaints.gov.au**
- National Aged Care Advocacy Program on **1800 700 600** funds the state-based aged-care advocacy services which are listed in Part 4. See also **myagedcare.gov.au/how-make-complaint/advocacy-services**

Chapter 12:
Ongoing care concerns

> 🖥 **myagedcare.gov.au**
> ☎ **1800 200 422**
> Advocacy ☎ 1800 700 600
> Complaints ☎ 1800 200 422

Over the months that follow Mum's health will inevitably change. Some things are to be expected as a normal part of the ageing process but there are other conditions for which you can get help. When information is offered in this chapter, it has always been taken from an informed source which will be quoted.

Depression

This topic has been included to encourage awareness of the potential for this problem. A proper diagnosis can only be made by a qualified practitioner but if you are aware of the symptoms, then you may be able to alert the staff or Mum's doctor when the problem might have otherwise gone undetected.

The following is taken from the Australian Institute of Health and Welfare's publication *National Health Priority Areas Report, Mental Health, Chapter 2 (1998)*.

A depressed mood is ubiquitous, common and generally lasts minutes to days. The individual feels 'down', hopeless, helpless, pessimistic, self-critical and has lowered self-esteem. Such moods may be quite severe, but by themselves are generally brief.

Depressive symptoms are given below and these represent a reasonable list of common features:

- depressed mood most of the day,
- loss of interest or pleasure (in all or most activities, most of the day),
- large increases or decreases in appetite (significant weight gain or loss),
- insomnia or excessive sleeping,
- restlessness as evident by hand wringing or similar activities, or slowness of movement,
- fatigue or loss of energy,
- feelings of worthlessness, or excessive or inappropriate guilt,
- diminished ability to concentrate or indecisiveness, or
- recurrent thoughts of death or suicide.

Some depressive episodes only appear for the first time in later life and depression in older people has been shown to be more likely to persist if untreated. Depression is often under-diagnosed in the older years.

The prevalence of depressive symptoms is strongly related to living arrangements for older people. Rates are lower among those who live in the community than among those in residential care. A 1997 survey found that older people in residential care experience about twice the level of depressive symptoms as those in the community and have a twenty times greater risk for major depressive disorders. Between 15% and 42% of residents in residential care homes experience a substantial level of depressive symptoms and between 6% and 18% exhibit depressive disorders. Depressive symptoms are also strongly related to physical health and loss of dear ones.

Rather than wait for depression to set in, it is far preferable to try and prevent it. The antidote to depression is activity. Firstly, the home will have a variety of activities some of which Mum will be interested in and you should encourage her to participate. But there may also be other activities that you can help her with or bring in when you come and visit.

If Mum is still mentally alert, then activities are almost more important. Like the rest of us she will continue to need mental stimulus, without which she will quickly get bored and lose interest.

Sadie's story

At 88, Sadie was struggling to manage at home and eventually her family moved her into care. Sadie's mental faculties were still extremely alert. For years she had done the daily paper's cryptic crossword and moving into care was not going to stop this. High on her list of things to take with her was her dictionary and thesaurus. One year on, she was still doing them.

Lesson: Mental stimulation is a lifeline for all alert people including those in care homes.

Mistreatment

We would hope that the staff would always treat Mum as we would. But we have to recognise that they can have off-days, be short-staffed and therefore more rushed, that some residents can be more demanding so leaving less time for Mum. And there may be some emergency or crisis, all of which make extra demands on all staff.

We also hope that we have chosen a home where the residents are treated with respect and dignity so that no neglect, however minor or mild, would occur. However, over time the staff will change, the management or ownership may also change, with the result that neglect might creep in or become more prevalent.

Only by keeping a watchful eye every time you visit, can you continue to ensure that Mum is being cared for satisfactorily. On the other hand victims may suffer in silence in the mistaken belief that if they tell, nobody will believe them or the consequences might be even worse.

Mistreatment covers a wide range of situations. They can be unintentional actions of a busy and hassled carer to the deliberate, premeditated behaviour of an opportunist or arise from the policies of management.

Whatever the situation, it would be appropriate to handle it carefully and delicately until you are certain of your facts. After all, in most cases Mum will have to go on living there after the issues are resolved. Every home has a complaints procedure but if you feel you need independent advice or support, there are also agencies that can assist you with this.

In an effort to prevent unsuitable people working in care homes, all staff and contractors must now pass a pre-employment police check. This also includes volunteers who have unsupervised access to residents.

Neglect

This is the last thing you would ever want to think about in relation to Mum, but sadly, you do need to be a bit vigilant. But let's put it into perspective. For every case reported in the papers, how many cases of excellent treatment do you never hear about? Thousands, I'd suggest. So don't rush into inappropriate conclusions just because Mum suddenly has a bruise. There may be a perfectly reasonable explanation.

Having said that, there is a neglect checklist in the Resources in Part 4 in case you feel there might be a problem. This list suggests things that you can look for. There may be other issues such as over-medication/under-medication that you can't easily identify.

Abuse

Elder abuse has been defined by the World Health Organisation as 'a single or repeated act, or lack of appropriate action, occurring within any relationship where there is an expectation of trust, which causes harm or distress to an older person.'

It can take the form of financial exploitation, intentional neglect or mistreatment by paid carers. The severity can range from simple ageist attitudes and disrespect to serious criminal actions. Be on the lookout for:

- excessive or frequent bruising,
- carers using the silent treatment,
- carers ignoring Mum or calling her inappropriate names,
- insults or threats, or

- misuse of her money or anyone preventing her having access to it.

Archie's story

Archie is a returned serviceman who receives DVA benefits and disability payments. Some years ago his wife passed away and he lived with other family members for a while before he befriended a lady through an off-chance meeting.

In due course Archie moved in to live with her and her family. Over time he was pressured to alter his Power of Attorney and will in her favour and she exercised considerable influence over him, under duress, including threats.

When Archie went into hospital the lady misappropriated a significant sum of cash that he held at home claiming it was a gift.

She also wanted to be appointed his carer so that she would receive government carer payments and potentially have a greater claim over his estate.

Archie was concerned about moving out from her home because he was worried about who would help him with his daily tasks, even though he was still able to live independently.

He finally sought help from his at-home care provider and his accountant who between them were able to find him accommodation at a Supported Residential Services home where he was able to apply for a CHSP to cover his needs. Archie also immediately took steps to alter his Power of Attorney and his will nominating people he could trust.

Lesson: Seniors do not have to live in a home environment which they are not comfortable with and are subject to unwelcomed attention or abuse. There are a number of

> alternatives and assistance packages available. A Power of
> Attorney and will can be altered at any time.

If you suspect abuse, initially you should discuss it with the DON. Keep a diary of conversations and actions and if necessary, take photos. If you need advice or an independent advocate, contact the advocacy service in your state or territory (see the Resources in Part 4).

If the matter is not properly resolved, you can contact Aged Care Complaints on **1800 200 422** or at **myagedcare.gov.au/financial-and-legal/how-make-complaint**. In the year to June 2010, 20% of the complaints raised to the Scheme were about abuse, and over 40% were to do with health and personal care.

If in due course, this still proves unsatisfactory, you can take your complaint to the Aged Care Commissioner on **1800 200 422** or at **agedcarecomplaints.gov.au**. Their website has considerable information about this process. Another website listing resources for help with all manner of abuse is **oneinthree.com.au**.

Reportable assault

A reportable assault is defined as unlawful sexual contact, unreasonable use of force or verbal or physical abuse in a threatening manner. All care homes must report all incidents of reportable assaults inflicted on residents to the local police and the Department of Health within twenty-four hours of the alleged incident. A missing resident must also be reported to the local police.

The home has the discretion not to report an incident if all of the following can be met:

- the resident who is alleged to have committed the assault is confirmed as suffering from mental or cognitive impairment, and
- the home sets up a behaviour management programme for the resident within twenty-four hours of the allegation being made.

Although this sounds fairly straightforward, there are situations which are not so clear-cut. For example:

- where verbal and financial abuse is alleged — this is not covered,
- when no staff member observes the alleged incident, or
- when a resident with mental or cognitive impairment reports alleged inappropriate behaviour.

Despite this, all homes must have policies and procedures for mandatory reporting which includes an obligation on all staff to report any incidents to their management and keeping consolidated records of allegations and incidents.

End of life care

As you might expect the majority of residents die in their aged-care home and we would all want to believe that Mum passed in pain-free comfort. Nursing for end of life has become a specialist skill called palliative care which is now recognised as the norm for all end-of-life care.

It is defined by the World Health Organisation, and in Australia there is both legislation and guidelines for managing palliative care in residential homes. The accreditation standards also require homes to manage symptoms and pain and to ensure that the resident's comfort and dignity is maintained at all times.

Palliative care aims to improve the quality of life for people towards, and at the end of, their lives by reducing suffering through the management of their pain, physical, cultural, psychological and spiritual needs. It also provides a support system for the resident and the family during the end times and the subsequent bereavement.

An open approach to discussions about death and dying between the staff, Mum and the family make it much easier to identify everyone's wishes regarding end-of-life care. This can allow Mum to stay in her familiar environment and to feel supported, safe and comfortable.

The general perception of palliative care is often that it is only relevant right near the end. But if Mum is, for example, a cancer sufferer and her symptoms include pain that gets progressively more debilitating, then palliative care methods should be introduced early on to improve her quality of life possibly even extending it.

In 2010, an American study of newly-diagnosed lung cancer patients found that those patients who had been given early palliative care treatments actually lived three months longer and also enjoyed a better quality of life, compared with patients who only received the standard treatment.

The other side to palliative care being applied in the care home is that it may mean that Mum does not have to be moved to a hospital or hospice near the end. Another study (also in 2010) showed that those who died in hospital experienced more physical and emotional stress than those who died at home with palliative care.

The *Guidelines for a Palliative Approach in Residential Aged Care* provides guidance for the delivery of a palliative approach in residential aged-care homes across Australia and all homes have a copy. More details from Palliative Care Australia at **palliativecare.org.au/home.aspx**. Other websites which might be helpful include:

- **dyingtounderstand.com**
- **centreforpallcare.org**

Towards the end

Even though this will be a difficult time, if you can make some practical preparations in advance then this is going to help you in the long run.

The home will already have Mum's Advanced Care Directive which should answer these questions:

- who to contact when death is close (including mobile phone numbers),
- what are acceptable times for contact, (do you want to be phoned at 3am),
- whether any special music is required,
- does Mum wish to be dressed in any special clothing,
- are there any religious requirements (last rites), or
- should they remove Mum's rings or other jewellery after death?

However you may want to reconfirm Mum's requirements

with the home as the end approaches. If she has been a resident for a long time, her wishes may have changed.

The home may want Mum's room cleared out within twenty-four hours of her death. This is obviously going to be particularly stressful at such an emotional time so anything you can do in advance is to be recommended:

- start removing some of her belongings. This is more appropriate for things like photos, valuables, items of sentimental value that you wouldn't want to lose.
- take in a suitcase or two for packing up Mum's belongings. In the heat of the moment and often at short notice, this is not something you are likely to think about. (If you haven't done this, her effects could end up in a plastic garbage bag in a store-room — she deserves better.)
- when you are packing up her belongings, remember to check pockets and lapels for small items like brooches and watches, before you ask the staff because you assume they are missing.
- the home may require that Mum's furniture is collected within twenty-four hours. If you are unable to do this, they may be at liberty to move it.

After death

Once Mum has died, the home will call the doctor for confirmation and the paperwork. They will then call your designated funeral director who will arrange to move her body to the funeral home.

You will be asked to pack up Mum's possessions as soon as possible. If you are unable to come immediately they may pack them for you and store them until such time as you can collect them.

Staff will assist you if they can but be prepared that this is a time when the practical efficiencies of running a home has to work side by side with grieving and emotional relatives. If you can't face doing it yourself, either get a friend or other family member to do it or ask the staff to do it for you. Whilst all this will surely feel cold and commercial, the home's interest now lies in admitting the next resident. They have done all they can for your Mum and it is now someone else's turn.

If Mum has been a long-standing resident then don't forget to advise the home (staff and other residents) of the funeral arrangements, as many of them will have become fond of Mum. Like relatives, staff also need the opportunity to grieve. If any special carers weren't on duty when Mum died, they would have missed the chance to say goodbye.

Peter's story

My Mum was a resident in a country-town nursing home for several years before she died. In the months near the end of her life she had trouble sleeping.

One particular night nurse realised this and in the small hours, she would sit with Mum. Over those months they had many long conversations about the changes that occurred during her nine decades of life. Very quickly this nurse became a special friend.

In due course Mum died. By the time this nurse came on duty at 11pm, Mum's body and her belongings had been removed. What opportunity was there for this dedicated nurse to say goodbye to her now-friend? Fortunately, she was able to attend the funeral to give her own good-byes. But before this, I didn't know that this wonderful friendship even existed.

Lesson: The night staff may well contribute more than you ever know to Mum's well-being, so don't forget them.

If you used a placement service to find the home, don't forget to tell them. They are always interested to hear how their placements are getting on.

If you feel that Mum has been well looked after, a formal thank-you note and perhaps a gift (like flowers, chocolates or a donation) for the home is always appreciated as an acknowledgement. And don't forget the unseen but equally important night staff. How often do all these carers, who deputised for you for the duration of Mum's stay, get forgotten?

Strictly speaking individual staff members are not allowed to accept personal gifts or legacies. If you wish to acknowledge a particular individual then you are more likely to have the gesture accepted if you do it out of working hours. Meeting a staff member for coffee or lunch for example, may well be accepted in the manner in which it is offered.

Jane's story

Jane's mother ended her days in a very caring supportive home. A few days after her death, her brother shared the home's lift with the catering manager. When he asked after Mum and was told she had passed away, he turned his head and could not speak. Through the tears he said what a beautiful lady Mum had been and how he would miss her.

This was a depth of feeling that we hadn't expected. Just

knowing that she was surrounded by people who genuinely cared certainly helped the family in the healing process.

Lesson: Don't under-estimate the impact that a resident may have on the staff nor how much they might care.

Chapter 13:
Dementia

> 🖥 fightdementia.org.au
> ☎ 1800 100 500
> 🖥 start2talk.org.au

Dementia is now the single largest medical condition for all newly admitted residents — two-thirds of all new admissions in 2014. Because of the nature of this condition, there are a number of additional issues that need to be addressed. Everything that has been written elsewhere applies equally to people living with dementia and this chapter adds some extra, dementia-specific considerations.

What is dementia?

Until we are confronted by dementia, most of us tend to think that a sufferer is perhaps just a bit forgetful. But it can be much more than that. According to Alzheimer's Australia, dementia is a term 'used to describe the symptoms of a large group of illnesses which cause a progressive decline in a person's functioning… including loss of memory, intellect, rationality, social skills and what would be considered normal emotional reactions.'

People living with early-stage dementia may be able to cope in a general aged-care home. However as the condition deteriorates, some or all of the following problems may mean that a specialised dementia facility is needed:

- propensity to get lost,
- be disturbed at night,
- wandering outside, sometimes at night,
- seeing or hearing things that are not there,
- become angry or aggressive,
- lose their ability to understand or use speech, or
- have uncontrolled movements.

There are many other symptoms and each person will have individual needs. For comprehensive and up-to-date information, advice and support, see the Alzheimer's Australia website at **fightdementia.org.au** or phone their National Dementia Helpline on **1800 100 500**.

Deciding on residential care

As with all decisions relating to moving a loved one into care, this is a particularly stressful and difficult process. You need to start with an ACAT assessment (see Chapter 4) to determine whether Mum requires residential care. You can then find a list of homes providing the special needs of people living with dementia, on the myagedcare website's home-finder page. You and the family can discuss any concerns or issues that you may have with the ACAT team. Although your choice may be limited to homes with specialist facilities, there are increasing numbers of homes providing dementia care.

Specialist dementia homes or units

While general aged-care homes can cater for residents with some degree of dementia, others provide more targeted dementia services. These homes generally have specialist staff and separate units or wings that have been specifically designed for a person living with dementia who may not otherwise be safely accommodated in a general care home. They will have noticeably higher levels of physical security both in the buildings and around the grounds. This is not for any imprisonment-type reasons, but rather to protect those residents who are prone to wandering.

There are many factors to weigh up when you are assessing aged-care homes. A general checklist is given in Part 4 plus an additional list with dementia-specific criteria. You should use both of these lists if possible. There is support and advice available from Alzheimer's Australia's website at **fightdementia.org.au/services** or from their National Dementia Helpline on **1800 100 500.**

It's also possible that your preferred home will not have a vacancy. If this is the case try not to be pressured into accepting just any offer you receive and keep in touch with your preferred home in case a place should become available. But you need to balance a choice to move into a less preferred home with the fact that people living with dementia don't accept change easily so having to move Mum twice may not be the optimal solution.

Planning for the move

People living with dementia can be disturbed by change, so if possible introduce Mum to the new home gradually, so that the environment becomes a little more familiar and less confusing and frightening.

Sometimes this is simply not possible, especially if the move has to be made quickly, but even then, it's important to emphasise the positive aspects of the move, such as the possibility of making new friends and enjoying new activities. Over time and with careful planning and sensitive handling, you should find that Mum will make the adjustment. If you have concerns about the move, talk to the DON.

Legal issues

As dementia progresses, Mum's ability to make legal and financial decisions decreases and in due course family, friends or a legally appointed person or organisation will need to take over. Ideally, wills, Powers of Attorney and such like should be addressed while Mum is still competent to make these arrangements for herself. Laws vary between states and territories, so it is important to contact a solicitor or the Guardianship Board in your state or territory for specific advice. Contact details are listed in the Resources in Part 4.

Definitions of the following items are given in the Glossary but there are extra considerations for people living with dementia.

Powers of Attorney

If an Enduring Power of Attorney is signed after the onset of dementia, a doctor who specialises in old age (a gerontologist) may be required to certify that the person living with dementia understands what is being proposed. A solicitor will take this into account when giving advice about the Power of Attorney.

Carers should also consider arranging an Enduring Power of Attorney for themselves, to ensure that their affairs are well managed if they are also unable to make decisions, either for themselves or for the person they care for.

Administrator

Mum may need an administrator, financial manager or estate manager if she is unable to manage her own legal and financial affairs due to any form of mental or physical incapacity. If she has not previously made a relevant Enduring Power of Attorney and any of these situations arises, then an administrator will be required to look after Mum including these situations:

- selling or leasing any real estate,
- when the bank signatories operate Mum's account,
- making sure she is not being financially exploited,
- making sure she is not suffering because of mismanagement of her funds,
- attending to other legal documents, or
- managing her investments.

If you have problems in dealing with the affairs of a person living with dementia, or if there is conflict in the family about their best interests, you can contact your local carers association (see the Resources) to discuss whether you might need the services of the Guardianship Authority in your state or territory. In some states and territories other formal arrangements are available, including medical guardianship and enduring Power of Attorney (medical).

Money matters

Planning money matters ahead means having joint signatures on all bank, building society and credit union accounts, discussing financial affairs with a financial adviser and arranging how and when the person living with dementia will access their finances. You can get help to plan ahead from an appropriate member of the bank's staff, an accredited financial adviser, your family solicitor or a public advocate.

If a bank account is in joint names (either to sign), the partner of the person living with dementia can continue to operate it without any change in arrangements. However, problems can occur if the person living with dementia uses the account inappropriately or has accounts in their name only.

To avoid these difficulties, the person living with dementia can, while still legally competent, give authority to another person to operate the account. If they are unwilling to agree to this, try talking to the bank manager about a possible solution.

Moving in

All the suggestions given in Chapter 9 apply equally well here. For people living with dementia it is really important to try to move Mum's furniture and belongings before you take her to the home. This will make the room feel more like her old bedroom and go some way to reducing any confusion or disorientation. Family photos, familiar prints, paintings or bed covers can all help.

You also need to recognise that it will take quite some time for Mum to adjust. This may not be easy for you and many carers visit frequently during this period, while others take the opportunity to recover from the stress of care-giving. There is no rule about how many times you should visit or how involved you should be in her care. But don't lose sight of your own needs along the way.

Good care

There are certain standards that apply to all residential care homes and these are largely defined in the accreditation standards (see Chapter 7). However, there are additional issues that need to be considered for dementia residents:

- care staff and management need specialist dementia-care training,
- physical environment designed for dementia needs including a safe wandering area,
- access to psycho-geriatric services,
- individualised care plans,
- culturally appropriate care,
- involvement of relatives and friends,
- effective pain management, and
- using minimal restraint.

If you feel that the home is not responsive to Mum's needs or that you're not getting the level of care you expect, talk to the DON and/or Mum's doctor first of all. Also have a look at the Resources in Part 4. If these don't resolve your concerns, then you can get more support by contacting:

- Aged Care Information Line on **1800 500 853** who will tell you about advocacy services in your state or territory,
- National Dementia Helpline on **1800 100 500**, or
- national advocacy services for your state or territory listed in the Resources in Part 4.

Suggestions for visits

Although visits can become harder as Mum deteriorates, there are many ways to make your visit pleasurable for both of you. For example:

- read newspapers and mail together,
- play games, listen to music or videos that she used to enjoy,
- revisit old photo albums,
- help out with personal care, like brushing her hair or doing her nails,
- go on a short outing or visit another resident in the home, or
- try holding her hands, massaging or strolling around the grounds.

Sometimes Mum will not want you to leave. If this is the case you can try diverting her or announcing when you arrive that you can only stay for an hour. It may also be helpful not to extend your goodbyes. If you are concerned, talk to the DON.

It's not uncommon for new residents to want to go home. If this happens, acknowledge her feelings and reassure Mum that she will be safe where she is. Try distracting her with another activity, but if possible, don't disagree with her.

Your new role

Although you have now stopped doing the physical tasks, there still are many ways that you can continue to help Mum. After all, you're the person who knows most about her needs, so you're well placed to work in partnership with the care home to advise and recommend.

To ensure that she receives the most sensitive care, you may wish to offer the home some details about the family background and information on her likes, dislikes and preferences. You can also help develop and review a care plan and ask to be consulted if there are any changes in behaviour. You can also expect to be consulted about daily living issues, be invited to read their notes and to attend meetings about the running of the home.

Taking care of yourself

After the move, you may feel relieved, guilty or just sad, and your daily routines will have changed, sometimes quite dramatically. During this period, it's important that carers take care of themselves and accept support from family and friends. You may also wish to call the National Dementia Helpline on **1800**

100 500 if you need someone to talk to. Homes may also run support groups for relatives as they recognise the difficulties of the move and try to make things as easy as possible.

More information

The following list is not exhaustive and the families of other residents may prove helpful because of their prior experience. You could ask at the Residents and Relative Group but also try:

- your doctor,
- your local community health service,
- National Dementia Helpline, phone **1800 100 500,**
- Aged Care Information Line, phone **1800 500 853**, or
- Commonwealth Respite and Carelink Centre in your state/territory (see the Resources in Part 4).

There are also a number of excellent websites with information and support facilities some of which are listed in the Resources in Part 4.

PART 3

Financial stuff

Top Tips for the financials

- Make lists of your financial assets and income.
- Work out how much lump sum you can pay for entry.
- Think about what you want to do with your home.
- Seek financial advice regarding what you can afford and how you can best pay for it.

Chapter 14:
Fees and charges

Now that Mum has had her ACAT assessment the next step is to prepare for, and then request, a financial assessment. This process is not accessible through the myagedcare website. It is a formal process undertaken by Centrelink (or the DVA) and is an analysis of Mum's income and assets. This information is used to determine what her aged-care costs and fees will be. She can choose not to do this (and you can skip Chapters 14 to 17) but she will then have to pay the required RAD plus the basic daily care fee and the maximum means tested fee.

This and the next four chapters will step you through the financial issues but first you and Mum will have to do a lot of homework to prepare the information you will need for completing the financial assessment form.

Without compromising the quality of her care, you have four financial objectives here. You need to organise both her assets and her income in such a way that you:

- minimise the cost of her aged-care fees and charges,
- maximise the value of her remaining assets,
- make sure that she will have sufficient income to cover all her living expenses including the new aged-care fees, and

- don't compromise her Centrelink/DVA pension and benefits.

Even with the most straightforward of financial circumstances, these objectives are not easily or obviously achieved. If Mum owns her own home, then this is the main trigger for considering professional help. At a minimum you can get limited free advice from a Centrelink Financial Information Service Officer (phone **132 300** for an appointment).

John's story

John is a specialist aged-care financial advisor who sees many clients coming for advice after they have sold Mum's house. In the majority of cases they would have been financially better off renting the house out rather than selling it. They could have discovered this if only they had sought expert financial help right at the start of this process.

Lesson: Don't under-estimate how beneficial professional advice can be and don't leave it too late. The benefits you can gain can far outweigh the cost.

These chapters are rather complicated and are therefore structured in logical steps to make it as easy as possible to follow. The goals are to:

- guide you through the preparation so that you can achieve Mum's objectives above,
- prepare you so that when you get professional financial advice, you will understand the options and strategies that might be suggested, or

- if you choose not to take outside advice, you are able to complete the assessment form in such a way that you can achieve her objectives.

In order to reach these end points, all the different aged-care fees and charges will be explained in this chapter. How income and assets are treated is discussed in the next chapter, followed by a complete chapter on the complex issue of what to do with Mum's home. Then the actual calculations are explained and illustrated, with a final chapter covering an assortment of other financial issues including the dreaded tax consequences.

Only some of this detail will be applicable depending on Mum's circumstances and level of care. This section (indeed the whole book) is not intended to be a DIY instruction manual; rather it provides guidance and advice from experienced experts on the financial aspects of the whole process.

A few definitions and explanations

Let's start with a bit of background to help you to understand the bureaucracy.

The DHS sets the rules and costs and is responsible for the aged-care system, whereas Centrelink or the DVA are the organisations that look after Centrelink pensions and DVA benefits. Centrelink or the DVA assesses Mum's assets and income on behalf of the DHS.

If Mum is a Centrelink pensioner or is not a pensioner at all, her contact for aged-care assessment purposes will be through Centrelink. If she is a DVA client all her dealings will be through the DVA office in her state or territory.

The DHS increases all aged-care fees and charges on 20 March and 20 September every year. The figures quoted throughout this book are applicable as at 20 March 2016. Check on the Centrelink or the DVA websites for the up to date figures.

Now let's define a resident. Because major changes to the whole aged-care system came into effect on 1 July 2014, this is a critical date. Everyone who had entered a residential home before 1 July 2014 is known as a continuing care resident. They will continue to be assessed under the old financial rules which remain in place. Generally speaking, the old rules are more financially favourable and as far as possible these residents should aim to retain their status which they will do provided they:

- do not leave the aged-care system for more than twenty-eight days in a year, or
- have not changed aged-care homes and have not elected to fall under the new rules.

As a result, in true bureaucratic style, there are two aged-care fee systems running in parallel, one for those who were permanent residents before 1 July 2014 and a different one for those who entered after this date.

First steps

Let's move on to the current rules that now apply to every new resident. Before getting into the detail, broadly speaking you will need to:

- familiarise yourself with all the possible fees and charges,

- make separate lists of Mum's assets and debts, income and outgoings, and
- investigate where you can get professional advice if her situation is the least bit complicated.

This is all in preparation for completing the *Residential Aged Care Request for a Combined Assets and Income Assessment* and then lodging it with either Centrelink or the DVA. Based on this information the DHS will determine which type of accommodation payment will apply, how much the means tested fee will be and in due course, they will advise both Mum and her chosen home.

This form refers to the 'relevant date' which is the date of permanent entry into residential aged care. It stands to reason that in most cases the form can't be completed until Mum has found a home and has either moved in, or has agreed to move in at a future date, and all negotiations regarding entry charges have been finalised.

The first thing we will look at is the fees and charges. Then we will go on to discuss how to tackle Mum's situation with a view to minimising her costs. Try not to get too stressed or overwhelmed as you work through all this.

Entry fees

Homes basically need to cover two different types of expenses: the cost of providing and maintaining the buildings and amenities, and their labour and operating costs in caring for the residents. As a result there are two different types of costs, up-front entry charges called accommodation payments (to pay for the grounds and buildings) plus ongoing daily care fees (to cover daily operating costs).

Only accredited homes can charge these fees. Private homes that operate outside the federal system can set their own fees. If Mum cannot meet the financial criteria applying to her when she is considering moving into an accredited home, then special rules called hardship provisions may apply (see Chapter 18).

The accommodation payments are entry fees which pay for the bricks and mortar of the home and there are three different ways in which these can be paid:

- a lump sum payable on entry, or
- a monthly payment which is the interest due on any unpaid part of the lump sum, or
- a combination of lump sum and monthly interest payments.

Because the government's policy is that nobody should pay more than they can afford, there are three categories for these fees:

- for better-off residents the fees are:
- RAD (refundable accommodation deposit) — a higher lump sum,
- DAP (daily accommodation payment) — monthly interest-only payment on any unpaid RAD.
- for less well-off residents the entry fees are:
- RAC (refundable accommodation contribution) — a lower lump sum,
- DAC (daily accommodation contribution) — monthly interest-only payment on any unpaid RAC.
- for residents with assets less than $46,000 none of these fees will apply.

Then you have to ask, how are these phrases 'better-off' and 'less-well off' defined?

All new residents are classified as a self-funded resident, a partial low means resident or a low means resident. Which group Mum falls into will be determined by her level of assets and income. This figure then sets the amount and type of her aged-care fees and up-front charges.

- self-funded resident — anyone whose assessed income is above $60.49 per day is able to negotiate a RAD or a combination of a RAD and/or a DAP to suit their circumstances.
- partial low means resident — anyone whose assessed income is between $54.29 per day and $60.49 per day may negotiate a RAC or a combination of a RAC and/or a DAC to suit their circumstances.
- low means resident — anyone whose assessed income is below $54.29 per day will only be asked to pay a RAC or a DAC.

Of the whole fee structure, the RAD is the only somewhat flexible component. The funds that the home receives from government subsidies and Mum's fees are not enough to cover their ongoing expenses. Apart from taking a bank loan, the only other source of funding is the interest it receives from investing the RAD/RAC. Therefore the home is entitled to:

- retain any interest it earns once the lump sum is invested, or
- charge interest (this is the DAP/DAC) which accrues on any unpaid portion of a RAD/RAC.

A home may only use the lump sum to:

- pay for improvements to the physical environment of the home,
- repay any debts relating to the home,
- refund a RAD/RAC, or
- invest the monies prudentially.

Refundable Accommodation Deposit (RAD)

A RAD could typically be $550,000 for a single room although some homes also have suites where the RAD can be as high as $1.8 million. As you might expect a higher RAD is payable in inner city areas and for more generously appointed homes. Generally speaking, it is important to pay as much of the RAD as you can as soon as possible to avoid the interest.

All homes are obliged to advertise the maximum RAD they charge for each of their rooms along with a description of the room on the myagedcare website. This is in addition to the details they may have on their own websites.

A home cannot accept a RAD higher than the published amount. However they can accept something lower. This creates an opportunity to negotiate a lesser amount but any negotiation must take place before Mum moves in because once she is in, it is fixed. Once you have agreed a figure, it is almost impossible to go back later and renegotiate it even if her financial circumstances change. It may be possible to revisit the RAD if Mum changes rooms or moves to a different home.

Each home sets their RAD in their own way. For example, a home might say that a room of a particular size or amenity has a certain RAD whereas another room with less amenities or a less spacious layout has a lower RAD. When you are searching for a home, you can inspect each room that is available and match it to your budget and comfort needs.

Daily Accommodation Payment (DAP)

The DAP is the monthly stream of interest-only payments. Interest is charged on any part of the RAD which is not paid as a lump sum on entry. The interest rate is set by the DHS.

The DAP amount is calculated by taking the unpaid RAD amount, multiplying that by the government scheduled interest rate and then dividing that amount by 365 to arrive at the daily cost. At the time of publication the rate was 6.01%.

Let's say that Mum has agreed to pay a RAD of $300,000 but wants to pay it as a DAP. Then her daily cost becomes:

$300,000 x 6.01% = $18,300 / 365 = $50.14 per day

Refundable Accommodation Contribution (RAC)

The RAC is a lower lump-sum entry fee applicable to less well-off residents. The RAC amount will be calculated on Mum's assessed income and it can vary over time in line with any changes in her means tested amount. There is no RAC payable if she has:

- assessable assets below $46,000, and
- assessable income below $25,711.40 per annum for a single pensioner or $25,243.40 for an illness separated couple (for example, where one spouse is already in a home and the partner is still living at home.)

An aged-care home is not permitted to accept a RAD or a DAP

from a resident whose means tested amount is below $54.29 per day for a newly built or significantly refurbished home. If the home doesn't fall into that category, the maximum is $35.37 per day.

Daily Accommodation Contribution (DAC)

The DAC is the monthly stream of interest-only payments. Interest is charged on any part of the RAC which is not paid as a lump sum on entry. The interest rate is set by the DHS. At the time of publication the rate was 6.01%.

The DAC is calculated by taking the RAC amount, then multiplying that amount by the government scheduled interest rate and then dividing that amount by 365 to arrive at the daily cost.

Let say that Mum has agreed to a RAC of $50,000 then her monthly DAC payments will be:

$50,000 x 6.01% = $3,005 / 365 = $8.23 per day

Payment strategies

Mum can choose which of the following methods suits her financial circumstances and needs:

- pay all the RAD/RAC as a lump sum on entry,
- pay part of the RAD/RAC as a lump sum on entry and then pay a monthly DAP/DAC on the remaining unpaid amount, or
- pay all the RAD/RAC as a monthly DAP/DAC.

Let's look at these in more detail. To illustrate, let's say that

Mum has agreed to pay a RAD of $550,000; now we can see what happens under these different payment options.

Lump sum RAD/RAC

This is what it sounds like. Mum pays the whole amount on entry which avoids all interest charges. If she is waiting on the proceeds of the sale of an asset to be received, she can negotiate with the home to defer payment until the funds have come in but interest will accrue at a rate of 6.01% from the date of entry. Most homes prefer this option because they can invest the funds which will generate interest income for them.

If she moves or dies then the home must repay the entire RAD/RAC amount.

Monthly DAP/DAC

These can be negotiated if Mum doesn't have enough cash to pay a lump sum but has a high income. Let's say she pays no lump sum at all on entry. The home will then calculate the monthly DAP to be $2,754.58 which is the interest on the whole RAD.

This option may not be as attractive to a home since they do not receive the lump sum payment. If Mum wants to go into a home where there is a high demand for places, she needs to make her application as attractive as possible. One way of achieving this is to offer some amount as a lump sum on entry.

When Mum leaves or dies, there will be no refund because she has only been paying a DAP.

Combination of a RAD/RAC with a DAP/DAC

This is an option if, for example, Mum has to sell assets to raise the cash for the lump sum. Let's say she can pay $100,000 from her savings when she moves in. This will leave her with a final payment in the future of $450,000. Her finances allow her to pay a DAP of $2,253.75 per month which is the interest only on the unpaid $450,000.

If Mum dies or leaves before the final balance has been paid, the refundable amount will be the $100,000 lump sum paid towards the RAD only, not the interest.

DAP/DAC deducted from a RAD/RAC

Mum could ask the home to deduct the $2,253.75 per month from the $100,000 lump sum she has already paid until such time as the sale proceeds from her home have been received. The original $100,000 will slowly reduce over time because the DAP is being deducted from it. Therefore the monthly DAP amount will gradually increase reflecting the higher amount of interest being calculated on the increasing unpaid RAD balance.

When she moves or dies only the remaining balance of the RAD will be refunded.

Moving homes

When Mum moves to another home you can ask for the RAD/RAC to be repaid and then pay a new RAD/RAC at the new home. Alternatively, with the agreement of both homes you can transfer the RAD/RAC.

As we saw earlier a continuing care resident is someone who

went into a home before 1 July 2014. For a continuing resident, the amount of RAD payable to the new home will be limited to the amount of bond they originally paid after the former retention amount has been deducted. These residents cannot be asked to pay a higher RAD or RAC if they move from one home to another. If a continuing resident does change homes they may elect to opt into the new rules and as such their accommodation and care payments will be reassessed.

We also need to consider involuntary moves. A move is considered to be involuntary when:

- it is triggered on medical grounds, or
- the room becomes an extra-services room and Mum doesn't want to pay for the extra services, or
- the room is being refurbished, or
- the home is closing.

For continuing care residents, if the move, either from one home to another or from one room to another in the same home, is involuntary then they cannot be asked to pay a higher RAD/RAC.

However if the move is voluntary then the RAD can be higher or lower than the original amount. They will also have their means tested amount recalculated and the new accommodation and ongoing care fees will become payable.

Best method

If Mum is in a position to be able to choose you might want to think about which is the most beneficial method of payment. Factors to consider include whether:

- Mum has sufficient cash at the time to pay a lump sum RAD/RAC,
- investments or other assets have to be sold to raise the lump sum,
- there will be any capital gains tax to pay if assets are sold,
- she has sufficient time to raise the money before needing to move in, or
- her existing income is high enough to cover the DAP/DAC.

If Mum expects to be in the home for more than five years then paying the RAD in full on entry, or by a combination of RAD and DAP, could be the cheaper option. On the other hand if she expects to be in the home a short time, then a DAP could be the better option avoiding the necessity of finding a large lump sum.

On admission Mum is not required to tell the home how she intends paying the RAD/RAC, either as a lump sum up-front, as monthly payments (DAP/DAC) or as a combination of both. This decision can be made up to twenty-eight days after admission. However interest starts to accrue from the date of entry. The thinking behind this government policy is to prevent homes choosing residents on the basis of how much lump sum they intend to pay up-front.

Sometimes the payment of a higher lump sum at entry can result in a resident receiving a higher Centrelink age pension. Depending on which home you go to and the amount you pay can mean that the results might be quite different.

Jim's story

Jim was looking at homes knowing that fairly soon he would need to move into residential care. He had been a city broker and well understood the nature of negotiating. He discovered that asking about the RAD from different homes in his area brought very different answers.

When the time came to move, Jim recalled this and decided to negotiate the RAD before he had his assets and income assessment done so that the homes were not aware of his financial situation. By telling the home about and comparing the RAD being offered by other homes he was able to negotiate a RAD which was lower than the published figure for a room that he liked.

Lesson: Generally speaking, commercial pressures between homes keep the RAD competitive. However it is useful to ask the home at the outset what their policy is regarding setting their RAD and what the RAD is for a particular room.

Placement services can be helpful here — their local knowledge can also include realistic guidance about the extent to which the RAD can be negotiated in any home. If you aren't comfortable doing the negotiations then they may be willing to do this for you for a fee.

Care fees

All the above discussion about RAD and RAC, DAP and DAC has been about paying for the bricks and mortar of Mum's new home. This section now talks about the fees that relate to her ongoing care. The type and amount of care fees Mum will have to pay are determined by her financial means and the home she chooses. The current fees are:

- basic daily care fee — $48.25 per day
- means tested fee — up to $71.07 per day
- extra-services fee — $20-$120 per day

Basic daily care fee

This fee pays for all Mum's daily needs including meals, laundry and cleaning as well as nursing. It is set at 85% of Centrelink's single rate of age pension excluding any supplements. Since the care fee is linked with the age pension which is indexed and increases on 20 March and 20 September each year, then this means that the care fee is also going to increase on these dates. This fee is not means tested and it is the minimum fee payable to an aged-care home. Everybody pays this fee.

Means tested fee

The government's policy is that all residents should pay a means tested fee and that no resident will pay more than they can afford or more than the cost of their care.

The means tested fee is a top-up care fee that only applies to residents whose income exceeds a certain threshold; different thresholds apply depending on whether Mum is single or a member of a couple. Fees for married residents are based on half the couple's combined assessable income.

The amount is based on a calculation (see Chapter 17) of both Mum's income and assets. This fee has two important maximum values:

- an annual maximum capped at $25,939.92 ($71.07 per day.) Once she has reached the this amount she will not have to pay this fee for the rest of the year.
- a maximum lifetime cap of $62,255.85. Mum will typically reach her lifetime maximum in about thirty months.

If she prefers not to provide details of her assets or income then she should expect to pay $71.07 per day. Many wealthy residents, who would reach the maximum means tested fee if their finances were assessed, prefer to keep their financial information confidential and choose to not disclose their affairs.

Mum will not have to pay a means tested fee if she:

- receives a full Centrelink pension,
- was a permanent aged-care resident between 1 October 1997 and 28 February 1998 even if she has since moved to another aged-care home,
- is in respite care,
- has a dependent child(ren), or
- is in high care and is a former prisoner-of-war.

Means tested fees remain current for three months and are reviewed quarterly from the start of January, March, July and September each year. If Mum's assessed income at the end of a quarter is less than what it was at the start, then she should receive a refund of the over-paid amount. However she will not be asked to pay any arrears if her means tested fee is subsequently assessed to be higher. She will be notified of any changes and she is entitled to request a review if her circumstances have changed significantly. Means tested fees are also index-linked.

Georgina's story

Ivan had had dementia for some time and for family reasons an administrator had been appointed to look after his welfare and finances and they co-coordinated his entry into an aged-care home. Ivan was happy there but his daughter Georgina couldn't understand why it was costing so much.

A court ruling finally appointed Georgina to manage his affairs and as soon as she gained control of his banking, she sought professional advice about the aged-care costs.

Ivan was paying the maximum means tested fee which was excessive given his income and assets. When this fee was added to the basic daily fee the cost of his care was over $40,000 each year which was prohibitively expensive.

A bit of investigation revealed that the relevant paperwork had not previously been returned to Centrelink. This meant that Centrelink, quite correctly, advised the care home to charge Ivan the maximum means tested fee ($71 per day) whereas the correct fee turned out to be just $21 per day.

Georgina then requested that Centrelink reassess the fees that he had already paid and in due course they advised the home of the correct amount. They then refunded the overpayment which amounted to a staggering $20,000.

Lesson: Always ask if you think there is a problem.

Extra-services fee

An extra-services fee is an further fee that Mum will be required to pay if she moves into an extra-services home. This covers the provision of additional hotel-type services or lifestyle extras including higher standards of accommodation and increased entertainment and food choices.

These fees are set individually by the home and will vary depending on what services are on offer. There are no maximum or minimum levels. You should expect to pay between $20 and $120 per day.

These fees are often negotiable but if Mum chooses to go to an extra-services home, she will be obliged to pay this fee. She can't say that she doesn't want to receive the extra services and therefore not be charged.

Some homes are unbundling their extra services so that residents can choose which ones they want and only pay for those. There is little point in paying for a glass of wine with the main meal if Mum doesn't drink.

Chapter 15:
Assets and income

This is the start of getting Mum's financial assessment done and the first thing you need is an itemised summary of her financial situation. You need to look at assets separately from income. Once you have done this (and it will take time to collect all the information), you will have an overall picture as the basis for taking the next step.

However, the rules around what is included or exempt are oh-so complicated and the whole process can be a nightmare if Mum's situation is the least bit complex. The rules have been summarised in these chapters but the value of taking expert advice or consulting a financial adviser who specialises in this area cannot be emphasised strongly enough.

Mum's assets

If you are already thinking 'Mum doesn't have any assets and can't afford aged care,' when for her own survival she must get care, then don't panic. Cases of serious hardship are catered for under the government's hardship provisions (see Chapter 18) and the rules around fees and charges take this into account.

The first thing to be aware of is that there is one critical threshold that determines a number of things, and that is $46,000 in assets (including the value of Mum's own home). This figure is the minimum amount of assets that she must be left with after allowing for the payment of the RAD. This is to ensure that she retains some discretionary funds. This minimum amount doesn't have to be held as cash; it could be, for example the full value of Mum's home if she decided to retain this after moving into care.

This figure will be taken into consideration when determining whether Mum will either have to pay nothing or a RAD or a RAC. If her assets are less than $46,000 she will be entitled to receive the maximum government support for her aged-care costs and will pay no more than 85% of her age pension. If she has assets higher than this then planning will be required.

You need to make two detailed lists of all the assets that Mum owns. The first list is for personal assets which are generally excluded from the income portion of the means test. These are usually items that cannot be used to generate an income. The second list is everything else and these are known as financial assets which will be counted when assessing her income. The reason for splitting them up is that they are itemised separately when the financial assessments are done.

Personal assets are:
- home value above $159,423.20 (minus any mortgage),
- contents of the home and personal effects — at a value that Mum could expect to receive if she sold everything at a garage sale,
- car(s) — at a wholesale value,
- caravan, boat, trailer, holiday home,
- personal effects including jewellery,
- collections like stamps, antiques or paintings, or

- funeral bonds (up to $12,250 per person), burial plots and mausoleums.

Quite often the contents of a home have minimal value because the items are old and sometimes unsaleable in which case they may need to be donated to a charity shop, given away or thrown away.

Financial assets are:
- value of the home up to $159,423.20,
- amount of the RAD or RAC,
- cash/bank account balances (including building societies and credit unions),
- investments (including shares, managed funds, term deposits, gold bullion),
- superannuation funds (current value),
- investment property(s) including a portion of farms (value minus any mortgages),
- life insurance policies (surrender value),
- loans made to outsiders or family members,
- businesses,
- value of gifts made in the last five years over the maximum thresholds, and
- refundable portion of any retirement village entry payment.

You now need to get realistic current values for everything on the lists. Items like bank accounts are straightforward, but for things like holiday homes you can use the capital improved figure on the council rates notice. Once you've got these details together is a really good time to get that professional financial advice.

Assets assessment

Firstly, it is not compulsory to have an assets and income assessment. If Mum chooses not to provide her financial details, she can either go into a private aged-care facility or pay the maximum fees and charges in a government-supported home.

The next step is to complete a form called a *Request for a Combined Assets and Income Assessment*. This is a very long form (don't panic — lots of big print and white space on the pages) that asks for details of all Mum's assets. It can be downloaded from **humanservices.gov.au/customer/forms/sa457**.

It comes with an explanatory information sheet called *Information you need to know about your Permanent Residential Aged Care Request for a Combined Assets* which can be downloaded from **humanservices.gov.au/customer/forms/ci020**.

The assets and income assessment enables Centrelink (or the DVA) to work out what accommodation charges and care fees Mum will have to pay. You or Mum should complete this form if she has had an ACAT assessment and expects to be approved for permanent care. She does not need to do this if she is going into respite care.

All the financial assets listed above are taken into consideration when Centrelink/DVA calculates Mum's assets. However, there are some specific rules which are worth mentioning:

- a RAD is counted as an assessable asset for aged-care means-test purposes but are not counted for Centrelink/DVA pension purposes,
- Mum's home will be included as an asset for aged-care fee purposes up to a value of $159,423.20 unless a protected person continues living there. A protected person is a:

- partner or dependent child (under 16 or a full-time student under 25),
- carer eligible for an income support payment who has been living in the home for at least two years, or
- close relative (father, mother, sister, brother child or grandchild) eligible for an income support payment who has been living in the home for at least five years.
- complying annuities (or pensions) which existed before 20 September 2007 are either 50% or 100% exempt from the assets test. If they were started after that date they are fully included, and
- if one partner of a couple is entering into aged care, then 50% of the couple's combined assets is taken as the amount of the individual's assets irrespective of who actually owns them.

Mum's house

This is the single most important element in all the financial calculations and it is almost always Mum's largest asset. There are a variety of options around what to do with the family home when she goes into care and because the rules around it are complex, Chapter 16 is devoted to discussing all these issues.

Mum's income

We said earlier that Mum's main objective is to complete the income and assets assessment form in the most beneficial manner. Since we have now reached this point, you may be wondering why we are moving on to talk about income.

Well, Mum's assets are used as the basis for calculating her income and what we are going to discuss here, is just how that happens. Her income is a crucial factor in determining the amount of her means tested fee. By looking at this now, we are achieving the other objective of making you sufficiently savvy to talk to a professional adviser without being overwhelmed.

Firstly, if Mum is already a pensioner then Centrelink or the DVA will already know her financial circumstances. However, for the purposes of assessing her income, all Mum's sources of income fall into two types, assessable income and deemed income.

Assessable income is largely real, physical money received from things like pensions or rent, whereas deemed income is about interest that could potentially be earned from investments. We will look at both of these separately and then put them together to show you how they link up to make Mum's total assessable income.

Assessable income

Virtually all of Mum's income, including any Centrelink/DVA pension, is included as assessable income for age-care fee purposes. Assessable income is all income physically received from any of the following:

- salary, business profits,
- superannuation schemes and allocated pensions,
- Government service pensions,
- Centrelink income support payments (excluding supplements),
- DVA pensions for veterans and widows without qualifying service (excluding supplements),

- overseas pensions,
- rental income from any source, and
- compensation payments.

You might be wondering, but what about bank interest or income from dividends for example? Irrespective of how much Mum earns from these sources, they are dealt with under the deeming rules which follow next.

Deemed income

Deeming is based on the idea that bank accounts and other financial investments can and must earn a certain rate of return. This approach aims to stop Mum from investing her funds at a low or nil interest in order to reduce her assessable income and consequently her aged-care costs. It also effectively removes any benefit she might gain from lending her money to family or friends to try and achieve the same result.

Each year (on 20 March and 20 September again) the government reviews the level of interest rates that are available in the market and publishes a deeming rate, which is a percentage that is an average figure that Mum could reasonably expect to earn without taking on significant investment risk.

This figure is used to calculate the amount of income that a person's assets could be expected to earn if they were placed in interest-earning investments. This rate is then applied to Mum's financial assets. This notional income is her deemed income. You can see that this deemed income is not necessarily the same as the real income which she receives into her account, nor is it the same as her taxable income. Deemed income is calculated from the values of any or all of the following assets:

- value of the home up to $159,423.20,
- amount of the RAD or RAC,
- cash,
- bank, building society and credit union accounts,
- friendly society bonds,
- managed funds,
- shares and other securities,
- term deposits, loans and debentures,
- superannuation and allocated pension accounts,
- gold and other bullion,
- financial interest in businesses including farms,
- values of certain short-term annuities,
- financial interest in controlled family trusts, and
- gifts which exceed the allowable limits.

The only things that are excluded are any extra value in Mum's home above $159,423.20 and personal assets, funeral bonds, pre-paid funerals and any long-term annuities or pensions.

Mum's debts

Although the income and assets assessment form asks for details of any remaining debts, very seldom is this relevant. If Mum does have any debts in regard to her financial assets then deeming is worked out after the debt has been deducted. Home mortgage repayments are not considered debts for these purposes but should be considered when you are working out her cash flow.

Realistically if she has large debts you will probably have to sell something to repay them; her remaining assets and income are then calculated in the way we have been discussing.

Rules for veterans

Generally speaking, the rules regarding the calculation of fees and charges for DVA pensioners are the same for Centrelink pensioners. However, there are a few important differences:

- the value of Mum's assets will be assessed by the DVA not Centrelink. They will usually already have this information on file,
- when the assets assessment is completed the DVA will notify Mum in writing about the outcome. The letter will explain how her assets were calculated and it will also include details about her aged-care fees and charges,
- war widow/widower pension is exempt income for a widow/widower who is also a veteran with qualifying service, and
- DVA disability pension is exempt income for:
- veterans with qualifying war service,
- partner of veterans with qualifying war service,
- war widow/widower.

Mum's DVA disability pension will be assessed as income unless she is a war widow (or widower if Dad is the surviving partner) with qualifying service and receives a service pension.

A key issue for DVA clients is that because normally the entitlement to receive a DVA pension and the income support supplement are means tested, then if a DVA recipient sells their home and is left with surplus funds, these DVA income payments could be lost.

Alice's story

Alice was a DVA war widow pensioner who entered permanent residential care before 1 July 2014. She sold her home in a leafy suburb to cover her accommodation payment after which she was left with a significant surplus that she was proposing to invest. After seeking financial advice she discovered that even though she would keep her war widow's pension, she would lose her income support supplement. This would put a strain on her cash flow which she still needed for her ongoing costs.

The financial adviser recommended that if she paid a higher RAD and chose a better appointed room then she could retain her DVA income support supplement.

Lesson: Knowing the DVA rules is the key to ensuring the best financial outcome. Getting financial advice from an independent adviser and/or the DVA or Centrelink, is the only safe way to ensure you get it right.

Chapter 16:
Family home

Assuming that Mum is still living in her own home (regardless of whether that is a house, apartment, retirement village unit, granny flat or whatever) and that she owns it (even if she still has a mortgage), this will almost universally be her largest asset.

This is a bit of a double-edged sword when it comes to moving into aged care. On one hand she is likely to want to preserve it, or at least as much of its value as she can, to pass onto her family. On the other hand, for many people it is the only place from which the money for the accommodation payment can be raised.

You need to think carefully about what you are going to do about the house when Mum goes into aged care. The options are obviously either to sell it or keep it. If you keep it, you then have are several choices about what you can do with it.

If Mum wants to keep the house then the cost of the RAD or RAC will need to be found from other sources including from the sale of other investments or by borrowing. Alternatively, the family might be able to get together to fund all or most of the costs. If this can be achieved amicably, then this is one way of keeping a family home or holiday house for future generations.

Your choices of action are:

- sell it — brings possible family and inheritance issues,
- keep it and borrow against it — brings inheritance issues longer term,
- keep it and rent it out — brings tax and management issues,
- keep it and leave it empty — brings security and maintenance issues, or
- keep it for Mum's partner, dependent child, eligible carer or a close relation who is receiving income support payments to live in — brings possible cash flow issues.

Before we look at these in turn, it is important to understand that in most cases Mum's assets and income are treated the same way for aged-care fee purposes and Centrelink/DVA pension purposes. However the treatment of her home is different.

Under certain situations a home can be exempt from aged-care assessment rules. However for everyone entering residential aged care after 1 July 2014 the home will always be included as an assessable asset up to a value of $159,423.20 unless a protected person continues to live there. A protected person is:

- a partner or dependent child (under 16 or a full time student under 25),
- a carer who has lived in the home for two years and receives an income support payment, or
- a close relative (parent, sister, brother, child or grandchild) who has lived in the home for five years and receives an income support payment.

From here the rules gets more complicated:

- if a protected person no longer lives in the home it will not be exempt and the capped value of the home will be included in Mum's assets test assessment, and
- a carer doesn't have to have received the income support payment for the two or five year period to qualify, and
- an income support payment does not include a carer allowance but can include a disability support pension or Newstart.

Mary's story

Mary's daughter Jill wanted to enter the property market and buy a home but didn't have enough money. To cover the purchase and moving costs, Mary gave Jill $150,000 towards a $400,000 house which was bought in Jill's name. Mary would have a life interest in it and they would both live in it.

They later discovered that Centrelink had decided that Mary had gifted $70,000 to Jill because this was the amount paid over and above the value received by Mary.

Lesson: Family arrangements can be beneficial for both parties but these arrangements can't be seen as a mechanism to confer an unreasonably large benefit to the offspring.

Turning to how Mum's home will be assessed by Centrelink/DVA, the general rule is that if she decides to keep it, from the date that she enters permanent residential care, her home will be automatically exempt from her pension assessment for two years and she will be treated as an ongoing home-owner.

Except under special circumstances involving the payment of a DAP or DAC, any rent she receives will be assessed as part of her income under the income test. After the two years have passed her home will be an assessable asset and she will be considered not to be a home-owner. This then means that her assets test threshold is higher.

Sell the house

This can be the most practical option particularly if Mum is unlikely to ever return to live in it. The proceeds of the sale of the home are likely to exceed the cost of the RAD so the surplus can then be invested to provide additional income to cover her care and other living expenses.

However, you will have to tell Centrelink that the house has been sold. Once the RAD has been paid, any surplus will count towards Mum's assets and income, which is likely to result in a reduction in her pension.

If she wants to maximise her Centrelink pension, then selling the home and being left with a large surplus after paying the RAD may not be the best alternative. Mum may also have to pay income tax on any earnings from investments if her taxable income exceeds the relevant tax-free threshold. Any surplus from the sale will also be included in the aged care means tested amount.

On the other hand, if Mum sold her home and paid the RAD in full she would be saving the high interest charge that she would otherwise have to cover on an unpaid RAD balance. For example, she might be able to generate say 3% on an interest-earning investment. But if she does this and then defers the payment of the RAD, she should be prepared to pay interest on the unpaid balance at 6.01% pa. Leaving aside the potential increase in the value of her home, she would be financially better off paying the RAD up-front if her investment earnings (after tax) cannot match the cost of the interest (6.01%).

The cost of the RAD is not included as an asset for Centrelink and DVA age pension purposes.

Edith's story

Edith's Mum had had a stroke leaving her partially incapacitated and Edith had been caring for her at home. She had taken some long-service leave to do this but eventually had to return to work. As there were no other family members to take over the role, they reluctantly considered a care home. In time, Mum agreed to an ACAT assessment which approved her as a permanent resident

Mum's only asset was her house so she decided to sell it and use the proceeds towards the RAD so she could avoid paying the interest (DAP). She had lived in the house for over forty years and was, understandably, extremely reluctant to sell but she eventually came to realise that this was the best way forward.

Lesson: Because it is an acknowledgement of finality, it can be emotionally very difficult to sell your home. But this can enable Mum to move to a care home of her choice with considerably less financial worry about the ongoing costs.

Borrowing against the house

Conventional home loans that require regular monthly repayments are normally inappropriate as a source of funding for the RAD, because Mum no longer has the income from which to make any repayments. One solution is a reverse mortgage or equity release/unlock product.

These are loans that allow the borrower to access some of the equity in their house without having to make regular loan repayments. Most of them work on the basis that the loan is secured as a mortgage on the house and the interest that you owe is added each month to the amount you have borrowed. (This effectively means that you end up paying interest upon interest.) You must repay the loan when the house is sold or when Mum dies.

These products are only available to people aged at least 60, and often 65 or older and can work well in situations where one spouse wishes to continue living in the family home and the other is moving to residential aged care. These types of loans can also be structured to provide a monthly top-up income to help pay ongoing care costs when one spouse remains at home.

With any of these products, the amount of money remaining after the eventual sale of the property is going to be significantly reduced by the loan plus the accrued interest that needs to be repaid from proceeds of the sale. Before taking up any of these loans/products, you need to read the small print very carefully. You must also get independent legal and financial advice before proceeding and be able to demonstrate that you have done this.

You could also check to see if the financial institution or the broker is a member of SEQUAL (Senior Australians Equity Release Association of Lenders) at sequal.com.au. This is the peak industry body for equity release providers. The industry is well regulated with additional laws being introduced in 2012 particularly to protect customers if negative equity arises. In this situation the law limits the value of the negative equity to the market value of the home so that the borrower does not have to pay more than the value of the home.

ASIC's MoneySmart website (**moneysmart.gov.au/ superannuation-and-retirement/income-sources-in-retirement/home-equity-release**) gives considerable details about these types of products. There is also a calculator to work out how much your debt will increase over time (**moneysmart.gov.au/tools-and-resources/calculators-and-apps/reverse-mortgage-calculator**). Using this calculator is a very salutary eye-opener about just how high and fast these debts can escalate.

Paul's story

In his working life, Paul had been a banker and understood the intricacies of financial products better than most. His house was in a prestigious inner suburb and he realised that its value was likely to go on increasing well beyond the average. He liked the idea of leaving his home for the benefit of his children and grandchildren.

As time went on he became more frail and widowed and he accepted the idea of moving into a care home. But he was adamant that he wouldn't sell his home to pay the RAD. He understood that there were a number of ways of borrowing against the house in order to raise the funds he needed to go into residential aged care.

He opted for a reverse mortgage of $100,000 against the house and paid this towards the RAD. His home was valued at $900,000 so it was an easy loan for the bank to approve. His financial adviser calculated that this would be enough from which to deduct the DAP payments for the foreseeable future and that the interest that would accrue on the mortgage would certainly be less than the expected capital growth in his house.

Lesson: By borrowing against the house, the family was able to retain it and potentially benefit from its increased value later on.

Rent it out

There are two possibilities here — either rent it out commercially or let a family member move in and rent it at a reduced rate in exchange for taking care of it. The rent can provide Mum with additional income to cover her care expenses. However, there are income tax and land tax implications with either of these alternatives.

For the first two years that Mum is in residential care, her home is excluded from Centrelink age pension assets test calculations and she will continue to be treated as a homeowner.

However, by paying either a DAP or DAC when the house is rented, the value of the house and the rental income are both excluded from Centrelink's age pension assets and income tests for as long as the house continues to be exempted.

When her aged-care fees and charges are being calculated her home will be included as an asset up to the maximum $159,423.20 unless a protected person continues to live there.

Monica's story

At 89 Monica was still managing at home until a fall resulted in a broken pelvis. She was subsequently assessed as needing residential aged care. Her main income was her Centrelink age pension.

When she added up the basic daily care fee, means tested

fee and the accommodation payment she found that her income was not enough to cover all the costs.

Then she realised that if she rented her house out, not only would the rent help make up the difference but she had the added benefit of having the value of her home and the rent excluded from her assets test potentially increasing her pension.

Lesson: Most people think that they have to sell their home in order to be able to pay for residential aged care but under the right circumstances and with some expert financial advice, there is often another way forward.

From 1 January 2016 new aged-care rules apply for assessing Mum's rental income. If she entered a home after that date she will have to include the rent as part of her assessed income and generally speaking she will end up paying a higher means tested care fee. If she was already in a home before that date any rent will not be assessed and it is likely that the cost of her care will be lower.

Leave it empty

This is always an option although not a particularly practical one. An empty property is open to vandalism and squatters, deterioration and decay unless someone is looking after it. After two years Centrelink will change Mum's status from a home-owner to a non-homeowner and it will also consider the property to be an assessable asset for the income and assets tests, potentially reducing her pension and any other benefits.

It is quite common for the home to initially remain vacant.

This way the family has time to consider Mum's future requirements and what they think is the best course of action. To keep the home vacant and available for her to return to is also reassuring. If things don't work out in the first few months she could always consider moving back home.

When Mum goes into care in one city and the children live in another distant town, the family might leave the home vacant so they will have somewhere to stay when they visit.

Ray's story

Ray had lived alone for many years but in recent times was coping less well. Reluctantly he agreed to an ACAT assessment which came back as residential care with respite care as an option. His family saw that this was an opportunity for him to have some proper care for a set period and a way for him to see if he liked a particular aged-care home.

Ray was well aware that care homes were full of women and he agreed to respite on the conditions that he went to a home that had some other menfolk but also that his house was left exactly as it was so he could return. The family agreed and after a month's stay, he realised that life was not as lonely and was actually much easier than struggling on at home.

Lesson: Leaving your options open can make the transition easier and the resident may also feel that they have ownership of the decision.

Keep it for a partner or a dependent

If Mum has a partner, a dependent child, a carer or close relative who is eligible for income support and they continue to live in the house after she has moved into care, then the house will be excluded as an asset when any accommodation payment and means tested fees are calculated. This leaves the family home available for any of these people to continue living in it.

> **Anne's story**
>
> Anne and her husband had always been the carers for their disabled, now adult, son. As a result, Anne's health had deteriorated over the years now leaving her in need of residential care herself. Confident that her husband could continue to manage at home with the help of professional carers, she agreed to move into a home. Because both her son and husband remained living in the family home, it was excluded as an asset from her assets assessment.
>
> **Lesson: Despite needing to find the money for a RAD Anne did not need to sell her home and her fees and charges were lower because the house was excluded from the financial assessment.**

Granny flat

This is being included here because special rules apply. A granny flat is an independent flat or unit which is part of a larger property usually owned (or jointly owned) by another, often younger, family member. Mum lives independently in the granny flat but the family is on hand if support or help is needed. This arrangement can work especially well if she can also benefit from help at home.

If Mum is living in a granny flat, Centrelink does not apply any tests of age or family relationship, nor does it put a value on the support provided by the family. However, the financial consideration that she pays to the family can fall within Centrelink's granny flat rules. The value of a granny flat is the amount paid (or value of assets transferred) if she:

- transfers the title of her home, or
- pays for the construction and fit-out of new premises somewhere else, or
- purchases property in another person's name in return for a life interest in the accommodation.

If the amount paid or value transferred is excessive, it can reduce Mum's assets and the flow-on effect could be that she has deprived herself of financial assets. In this case, the excess amount can be added back to her assets in determining her Centrelink entitlements and later on, her aged-care fees and charges if she moves into a care home.

If it appears that the amount that Mum paid is excessive, Centrelink may apply a reasonableness test and value the granny flat at a lower amount than she paid. The excess will be treated as a gift and added back to her financial assets.

The granny flat rules apply when:

- Mum pays for a life interest or right to accommodation for life, and

- the accommodation is in a private residence that is to be her principal home.

The rules do not apply if she continues as an owner (or part owner) because she already has the legal right to live in the property because of her ownership.

De facto and same-sex couples

The same rules that apply to hetero-sexual couples in a marriage also apply to de facto and same-sex couples. Whether the relationship is deemed to be a de facto one or not, will be a question of fact not opinion.

A de facto relationship is defined as a relationship between two people who are not legally married, who are not related as a family and who have a relationship as a couple living together on a genuine domestic basis. A de facto relationship can exist between individuals of the same or opposite sex and even where one of the individuals is legally married or in a de facto relationship with someone else.

This has the effect that recipients of Centrelink and/or aged-care benefits who are assessed as being a member of a same-sex couple will be attributed with half of the total value of the couple's income and assets when determining aged-care fees and charges. This is irrespective of who actually owns the assets or generates the income.

If a home is wholly owned by an aged-care resident who is also a member of a same-sex couple then the value of that property can be excluded in the same way as it is for a heterosexual couple. This same resident may also be required to pay a RAD or a RAC because their partner's assets will be included and they are considered to be part of a couple. The higher couple assets test thresholds will also apply.

Chapter 17:
Doing the sums

Now that all the possible costs and how Mum's assets and income are used in the financial assessments have been explained, it is time to move on to look at the actual calculations.

The means tested amount (MTA) is the critical figure for determining the type and amount of Mum's accommodation payment as well as her ongoing care fees. This is calculated by adding her income tested amount to her assets tested amount so let's look at these first, starting with her income.

Income

The first place to start is with the deeming calculations. In Chapter 15 we saw that deeming is the idea of notional interest income that Mum could reasonably expect to receive from monies that are wisely invested.

This table shows the rate and asset values used by Centrelink that are effective at the date of writing. The thresholds apply to a single pensioner or a couple including de facto and same-sex couples. When one member of a couple receives the Centrelink pension but the other is not yet eligible, then the half-couple rule is used.

- Single pensioner: first $49,200 at 1.75%, and everything above that is 3.25%
- Pensioner couple: first $81,600 at 1.75%, and everything above that is 3.25%

To calculate the deeming amount, the values of all Mum's financial assets are added together. (You are likely to have this figure from her asset inventory.) Let's say that her total financial assets are $100,000 and she is a single person. Then you calculate it like this:

Step 1:	$49,200	x 1.75%	= $ 861
Step 2:	+ $50,800	x 3.25%	= $1,651
Step 3:	= **$100,000**		= **$2,512**

Therefore, Mum's total yearly deemed income is $2,512. If Mum's investments actually generate her with income which exceeds the deeming amount, then that will be her gain because the extra cash income is ignored when calculating the means tested fee.

Now let's assume that Mum also receives a pension from her superannuation of $10,400 per annum, in addition to her Centrelink age pension of $18,200 per annum. Her total assessable income becomes:

	Centrelink pension	$18,200
+	deemed income	$ 2,512
+	superannuation pension	$10,400
=	Total assessable income	$31,112

Mum's income tested amount is now calculated using this simple formula:

50% x (total assessable income — income free area) / 364

The total assessable income is the figure calculated above. The income free area is an amount that you can earn without penalty which is not included in the income tested amount. The income free amounts are:

- Singles: $25,711.40
- Member of a couple: $25,243.40

Using the formula from above, Mum's income tested amount then becomes:

50% x ($31,122 — $25,711.40) / 364 = **$7.42 per day**

Assets

Mum's financial assets are $100,000. Now let's also assume that she owns her own home which is worth $350,000. But for the purposes of calculating her aged-care fees, there is a cap on the house value which is currently $159,423.20.

So Mum's total assessable assets are:

	Capped value of the home	$159,423.20
+	**Mum's financial assets**	**$100,000.00**
=	**Total assessable assets**	**$259,423.20**

The assets tested amount is calculated using the following percentages:

Assessable assets below $46,000	0%
+ Assessable assets between $46,000 and $159,423.20	17.5%
+ Assessable assets between $159,423.20 and $385,269.60	1%
+ Assessable assets over $385,269.60	2%

For members of a couple, half of their combined assessable assets are included.

Therefore Mum's assets tested amount will be worked out like this:

	Assets		Amount
Between $0 and $46,000 =	$46,000	x 0% =	$0.00
Between $46,000 and $159,423.20 =	$113,423.20	x 17.5% =	$19,849.06
Between $159,423.20 and $385,269.60 =	$100,000.00	x 1% =	$1,000.00
Totalling	$259,423.29		$20,849.06

This equates to $20,849.06 / 364 = **$57.28 per day**

Means tested amount (MTA)

This is the crucial figure and is simply the sum of the income tested amount plus the assets tested amount. So Mum's MTA is:

$7.42 + $57.28 = **$64.70 per day**

Mum's ongoing care fee

In Chapter 14 the standard fees are shown as:
- basic daily care fee — $48.25 per day
- means tested fee — up to $71.07 per day

Having now calculated Mum's MTA (which is less than this maximum), her daily care fees will be:

	Basic daily fee	$ 48.25
+	Means tested fee	$ 64.70
=	**Total**	**$112.95 per day**

Chapter 18:
Other financial considerations

As with any complex system there are a few situations that do not arise in the normal flow of everyday life and these are covered here.

Hardship provisions

The government's policy on aged care says that all registered homes must have accommodation for those people who are in financial hardship. These are generally people who have few assets and do not (and often never have) own their own home.

The DHS administers the financial hardship provisions. You have to apply for this assistance and may have to provide documentary evidence. The application form can be downloaded from **humanservices.gov.au/customer/forms/sa461.** The DHS may take several weeks to process your application so if you need to have this approved before Mum moves into a home, you need to submit it many weeks, even a couple of months, in advance.

Applications will be considered based on Mum's total finances including any that are as yet unrealised. This may include things like her eligibility for a pension if she doesn't already receive one, or any assets which she has been trying to keep for her beneficiaries and therefore has not cashed in. If Mum is one of a couple, then the DHS will consider that half their combined income and assets is Mum's total worth.

Mum will not be eligible for financial hardship assistance if she has:

- not completed and lodged an aged-care income and assets assessment form,
- gifted more than $10,000 in the previous twelve months or more than $30,000 in the previous five years, or
- assets valued at more than $34,082 unless they are unrealisable.

An asset is considered unrealisable if she cannot sell it or borrow against it and may include the following:

- a house that has been on the market for six months or more,
- jointly owned property,
- gifts made in the past if the decision to make the gift was made when the person was incapacitated or was made by a Power of Attorney, or
- frozen assets.

Rented properties, private trusts and private companies are not considered unrealisable for financial hardship assistance purposes.

The DHS will generally consider a request for either a reduction in the daily care fee and/or the income tested fee or the up-front fees to a maximum of both fees being waived. Financial hardship assistance will not be granted for extra-services fees.

If Mum only needs low care, then going into an SRS home is another option. SRS homes generally do not ask for an upfront deposit and the fees can be negotiated.

On average, 25% of residential aged-care places are reserved for fully-supported residents. However, the reality is a bit harsher. If Mum's preferred home is quite small then it may only have one or two beds for fully-supported residents.

If Mum lives in a less-well-off area this is likely to be made worse because the demand for these beds is quite high. This means that the waiting times can be many months. From the home's point of view, the owners would rather have fee-paying residents. Therefore in theory yes, Mum can still get into a care home, but in practice it may be harder to achieve.

Reclaiming the RAD or RAC

There are three situations in which you would need to reclaim the accommodation payment

- Mum moves out of the residential aged-care system into home care, or
- she leaves her current home for any reason, or
- she dies.

When Mum elects to leave either because the home has asked her to leave or she has chosen to leave and has given the appropriate notice, the RAD must be repaid at the time of leaving. If no notice has been given then the RAD must be refunded within fourteen days.

When Mum dies the executor of her will must reclaim the

RAD. The home will ask to see a certified copy of probate and once this has been provided the home must repay the balance in fourteen days.

If Mum moved in after 1 July 2014 and the RAD was paid in full when she first moved in and there are no other amounts owing to the home, then the full amount is repaid. However, if she was paying a DAP which was being deducted from the RAD, the net amount will be refunded.

For continuing care residents the retention amount will be deducted from the bond and the balance repaid. This is $331 for each month of Mum's stay for up to a maximum of five years which comes to a maximum of $19,860. If the bond was being paid periodically then the payments cease once her room has been vacated. Since the retention amount was included in these periodic payments there should be no refund or payment on either side.

All the interest that Mum's bond has earned during her stay belongs to the home.

Payment guarantees

The number and size of payments made to government-funded care homes as up-front charges, whether the old accommodation bonds or the current accommodation payments, has risen enormously in recent years. In 2011 the Productivity Commission wrote that 'between 1998 and 2008, the average value of each new accommodation bond increased by 13 per cent per year.' By 2010 the average bond was 120% of its value only three years earlier in 2007.

All homes are required to refund the accommodation payment (or bond) when Mum leaves regardless of the reason.

But what happens if the home has gone bankrupt or is in financial difficulties?

Legislation was introduced in 2006 to protect bonds and the resulting system was the Accommodation Bond Guarantee Scheme. Updated legislation was passed in 2013 — *Aged Care (Bond Security) Amendment Bill 2013* — but this was largely to amend the terminology.

The Scheme guarantees that the government will repay a resident's accommodation bond (or payment) balances (including interest) if an approved home is bankrupt or insolvent and has failed to refund any outstanding monies. In exchange for the payment, the resident transfers all their rights to recover the amount to the government.

This scheme only applies to government-subsidised homes; private homes outside the federal system are not covered by this legislation.

Tax considerations

There are two opportunities where a tax benefit can be gained from borrowing to finance Mum's stay in her aged-care home. One is tax offsets and the other is loan interest. The potential downside however is capital gains tax.

Tax offsets

If Mum is required to lodge a tax return, she will be able to claim certain aged-care payments as a Net Medical Expenses Tax Offset up until 30 June 2019. Residential aged-care expenses that qualify include:

- basic daily care fees,
- income tested or means tested fees,
- extra-services fees,
- DAP and DAC,
- accommodation charges, and
- periodic payments of accommodation bonds.

Lump sum payments of accommodation deposits (RAD) or contributions (RAC) do not qualify.

These payments must be made to an approved aged-care home for the resident's care. This also means that residents who have chosen not to be assessed by ACAT may not be eligible for these tax offsets.

The Net Medical Expenses Tax Offset is calculated as:

- For single taxpayers whose adjusted taxable income is less than $90,000, (for couples it is less than $180,000) the amount to claim as an offset is 20% of the amount above the threshold of $2,265.
- For single taxpayers whose adjusted taxable income is higher than $90,000, (for couples it is less than $180,000) the amount to claim as an offset is 10% of the amount above the threshold of $5,343.

Loan interest

If Mum has had to take out a loan or conventional mortgage to pay for her up-front entry fees then the interest charged can be claimed as a tax deduction from her income. If, however, she has taken out a reverse mortgage or equity release product, this does not apply because she is not yet repaying any interest (because the interest is being added to the amount borrowed).

It may be possible to claim the interest at the end of the loan term providing Mum still meets the tax rules governing medical tax offsets. In other words, if her house is sold while she is still alive and the loan is fully paid out, then she may then be able to claim all the interest because she is still living in her care home.

Capital gains tax

If Mum sold her house when she went into residential care, there is no capital gains tax liability because her primary residence falls outside the capitals gains tax network. However if she has sold a holiday home or other assets that she acquired after 1985 and they have significantly increased in value, she will be liable for capital gains tax. This should be taken into consideration when the entry fee is paid to make sure that she still has sufficient cash to pay the tax.

If Mum decides to retain her home and rent it out, after six years it is likely that the primary resident's capital gains tax exemption will be partly lost depending on how long it has been held as an investment.

Land tax

If Mum decides to retain her home and even if she leaves it vacant or rents it out, since it is no longer her primary residence it is likely that the various state governments will levy land tax on its unimproved value.

Chapter 19:
Financial strategies

Almost everyone entering residential aged care will need to assess their financial situation carefully. Mum's primary objectives in this regard are to minimise the means tested amount by reducing assessable assets and, linked in with this, to reduce assessable sources of income so that you can preserve her assets as far as possible. These objectives should be balanced with the idea that she will need to retain access to some liquid funds to help towards her living costs or other unforeseen expenses. These are likely to exceed her government pension even if she has modest assets.

Since 90% of people entering aged care are age pensioners (either Centrelink or DVA) it is particularly important to organise Mum's finances so that her pension income and/or other benefits are not affected.

Eleven strategies are discussed in this chapter — these are typical, but certainly not exclusive and they are not in any particular order. Two or more strategies can also work together to improve Mum's and the family's situation. So cherry-pick from them to suit her needs and circumstances.

Variations and more complex strategies are all possible depending on her individual circumstances. But (and this bears repeating) if you are in the least bit concerned or confused (and you won't be the only one), get professional advice. You only get one chance to get this right — you can't go back and renegotiate the RAD or other charges later on or even more importantly un-sell Mum's home once it has been sold.

Strategy 1 — mixture of RAD and DAP

If Mum is unable to pay the RAD in full when she moves in she has the option of paying a mixture of a DAP with or without an initial RAD.

If Mum's only asset is her home which needs to be sold to pay the RAD, or if the sale of assets would cause hardship, she can ask the home if she can pay the RAD as a DAP. She would need to be sure that her other sources of income will be sufficient to cover her cash flow needs. Her income might be supplemented by the family (especially if they are keen for her to retain the home) or from income she receives from elsewhere. If she wants to keep the house for example, she could rent it out and the rent could contribute towards the payments.

Once a DAP arrangement has been agreed with the home, the DHS' current interest rate is applied. This remains fixed throughout her stay in the home. The DHS sets and reviews the maximum interest rate quarterly but this is then only applied to new residents.

Robert's story

When Robert was assessed as needing care he was determined not to sell his home. It had been in the family for three generations and with commanding sea views, it was irreplaceable. His daughter, now married with three children, had outgrown her own home and was very happy to rent it from him. He needed to rent it but didn't want to put strangers into it but knew that his daughter would look after it lovingly. So he negotiated with the care home that he would pay a large portion of the RAD on entry and the balance by a DAP which came from the rent.

Lesson: By paying the RAD as a DAP and by renting out his home, Robert was able to keep his family home for future generations.

If Mum has enough income-generating assets, she might choose a DAP as a deliberate strategy to maximise her finances. Most homes prefer a lump sum RAD but all homes must offer a DAP as an alternative. If for example, Mum's assets were tied up in the family business and to free up cash would cause hardship for the business, then should funds become available in the future, Mum could make ad hoc RAD payments which would reduce the monthly DAP payments.

Strategy 2 — pay a larger RAD

By law all homes must publish their maximum RAD on the myagedcare website. The law also stipulates that residents cannot negotiate a higher RAD than these published figures. However, if Mum paid a higher RAD for a better home or a better room, her Centrelink/DVA pension could be improved. This is because the RAD is exempt from both the income and the assets tests.

Diana's story

Diana, a Centrelink age pensioner moved into an extra-services home and was asked to pay a RAD of $550,000. She sold her home for $850,000 leaving her with $300,000 available to invest.

A financial planner suggested that if she was willing to pay a higher RAD for a better appointed room than the $550,000 for a basic room, there would be Centrelink benefits and aged-care fee reductions.

He calculated that the savings in the reduced means tested fee, together with the resultant increase in her Centrelink pension would bring a better lifestyle and financial outcome than investing the $300,000 elsewhere.

Lesson: Sometimes paying a higher RAD is the most advantageous solution.

Even though a RAD is included in the calculation of Mum's asset value for the asset means test for aged-care purposes, the amount paid isn't deemed for the income assessed amount, which may help Mum reduce the combined means tested amount.

Strategy 3 — income-friendly investments

Income streams such as annuities may be an alternative to retaining an investment which would be included in the deeming rules. This is because a portion of the income received through an income-stream investment will be a repayment of part of the original capital invested. This is called a deductible amount and it reduces the level of the assessable income which is included when the means tested fee is calculated.

Joe's story

Shirley sought financial advice regarding her father Joe who was living by himself in a retirement village. He had financial assets of $250,000 and the value of his unit was estimated at $380,000. He had recently been assessed as needing residential care and together they had found a suitable home. Joe had decided that he would sell his unit.

Joe's RAD was going to be $450,000 so he thought that he would deposit the surplus into a term deposit and have the interest paid into his normal bank account. The financial adviser suggested a more beneficial alternative. If he invested his surplus into an annuity this would provide him with extra guaranteed income, lower means tested fees, a good rate of fixed interest on his investment and improve his Centrelink benefits.

Lesson: Annuities can offer an alternative that provide a safe investment, reasonable returns, lower care fees and higher Centrelink age pensions.

Strategy 4 — create a trust

Setting up family and special-purpose trusts are another way of decreasing Mum's aged-care fees by reducing the level of her assessable income. These approaches work for families with higher levels of income and/or assets or families where these structures are already in place for estate and tax planning purposes.

Since the introduction of the 1 July 2014 changes, the creation of family trusts to hold investment bonds has become a popular strategy. Invariably this level of sophistication is tailored to individual circumstances and specialist financial planning and legal advice should be obtained before proceeding.

David's story

During his working life David was a doctor and he had carefully invested surplus funds for the future. He decided to set aside $300,000 into three separate investment bonds which were earmarked for his children. When he needed to move into aged care he sought advice about how to best structure his finances.

He was advised to transfer the ownership of the bonds into a newly created family trust so that these investments were not deemed. This didn't trigger any capital gains tax which made David particularly happy.

Lesson: Investment bonds can offer an alternative way of reducing assessable income and it doesn't always involve a new investment, merely a restructure of the ownership of existing investments.

Strategy 5 — sell other assets

If Mum has assets such as land, a holiday house or other investments, some of these could be sold to pay the RAD. Depending on which investments are sold there could be capital gains tax implications. By selling these types of assets there could be an improved Centrelink/DVA outcome.

Ewan's story

Ewan was a country vet and apart from his home, he and his wife owned a beach house which the family used for summer holidays. As the children grew up the house was used less frequently although its value had grown significantly.

After Ewan died, his wife Joan sought advice on how to fund the payment of a RAD ahead of her move into an aged-care home. She was surprised to learn that the holiday house was purchased before capital gains tax was introduced. If she sold this property she would have sufficient funds to pay the RAD.

Her age pension was also going to improve because the holiday home (an assessable asset for Centrelink purposes) was going to be replaced with a RAD (which was Centrelink exempt). And even more… no capital gains tax had to be paid. The RAD could be paid in full which meant that she wouldn't be charged the 6.01% interest on any unpaid balance.

Lesson: All assets should be critically reviewed when deciding how to fund the RAD.

Strategy 6 — repay debts

As we saw earlier, the family home is usually Mum's largest asset but it can also be exempt from Centrelink's assets test. If she still has a mortgage/loan on her home then realising some other assets or using cash to pay off part or the entire mortgage can achieve three things:

- preserve the full value of the property because the debt is lowered or fully paid out,

- reduce the remaining amount of other assessable assets. This potentially results in a reduced means tested fee, and
- preserve her Centrelink pension entitlements.

In other words, if Mum has debts and she is able to sell assessable assets to repay some or all of those debts, she may be able to optimise her financial situation provided the specific assets and debts are chosen carefully.

Strategy 7 — prepay funeral expenses

There are two funeral-related items that are exempt assets. These are prepaid funeral expenses and funeral bonds where money has been invested for the express purpose of paying for a funeral.

Any amount invested as a prepaid funeral is excluded from the assets test. The interest that is being earned on this amount is also excluded from the income and assets test. However, you need to balance how much the funeral is likely to cost against how much you need to reduce your assets — be realistic here.

Once the prepaid funeral or funeral bond is paid the money can only be released to the executors to pay for the funeral. If there is a surplus, the remainder is returned to the executors as part of the estate.

Funeral bonds are a bit more complicated. Firstly the initial investment must not exceed $12,250 per person. If you invested say $13,000, then the whole of that $13,000 would be included as an asset for assets test purposes. It doesn't work on the basis that the first $12,250 is excluded and only the balance is counted. Normally separate accounts are established for amounts over the maximum exempt amount to avoid this problem.

As funeral bonds earn interest, it is quite possible that the bond will exceed $12,250 in the future. As long as the initial investment was less than $12,250 then the whole amount remains exempt.

One way that a couple could super-charge this strategy would be for each person to invest the maximum amount of $12,250 in bonds giving a total reduction in the couple's assets of $24,500.

Strategy 8 — gifting and estate planning

This means giving money, an asset or financial assistance as a gift. This has the effect of reducing Mum's assets and therefore her income. The Centrelink rules say that she can gift up to $10,000 each year or up to $30,000 in a five-year period to remain within the assets test exempt band. (Be careful she doesn't overlook things like financial assistance for children's or grandchildren's private school fees which can be substantial.) When she does this, you or she should advise Centrelink (or the DVA) so that the impact on her pension entitlements can be reassessed.

> ### Joy and Harry's story
> Over forty years of married life had meant that Joy and Harry had accumulated significant investments including a substantial family home. They decided that when they died they would leave their individual estate to the other and they had made wills to this effect.
>
> When Harry entered a care home, their total combined assets were assessed with half being apportioned to each of them. Harry's care-home costs were then calculated on his half which resulted in an affordable level of fees.

However, it then occurred to them that if Joy should pass away while he was still in the home, then his fees would increase significantly because their income and assets would no longer be assessed half and half. After getting some professional advice, they restructured their investments and rewrote their wills leaving their assets to other family members.

Lesson: To ensure that aged-care fees remain affordable, firstly seek professional advice and also reconsider who the beneficiaries in your wills should be.

Strategy 9 — reduce the value of assets

As we saw in Chapter 17, Mum's income is calculated using the deeming rules based on the value of her assets. Therefore if she can reduce the value of her financial assets, she also reduces her income. This can potentially improve her Centrelink/DVA pension and benefit entitlements as well as reducing her daily costs for care.

One way of doing this in the past has been to invest (from cash or other assessable investments) in complying income streams (meaning an investment which pays an income and is either fully or partly exempt from the assets test).

Complying income streams include certain annuities and pensions that were taken out before 20 September 2007. Any new ones started after that date are not eligible but pre-existing ones continue to retain their exempt status. If Mum had taken out an annuity before this date then it should be left undisturbed if at all possible.

Strategy 10 — staggered entry for couples

If both Mum and Dad are thinking about moving into a care home, they should consider making two separate moves if they can. When the first one moves, their accommodation payment and means tested fee will be calculated excluding the family home because their spouse is still living there. When the second one then follows, the family home will be treated under the normal rules and assessed up to the maximum of $159,423.20. Staggering entry will generate lower costs for one of the couple and possibly higher Centrelink age pensions.

In recognition of the financial impact of both Mum and Dad moving into care at the same time, some homes make special financial allowances in regard to the RAD to make it affordable.

If one partner is living separately from their spouse due to illness (including the need for residential care) leaving the other spouse still living at home, higher Centrelink benefits are payable under the illness separated couple rules in recognition of the increased costs of two people living apart. This rate also applies when both members of a couple move into permanent residential aged care and into separate rooms.

> **Charlie and Louise's story**
>
> Charlie, 79, and Louise, 81, had been married for over fifty years and for the past few years Charlie has been looking after Louise due to her severe dementia. This was taking its toll on his health and when he reluctantly accepted the idea of moving into care there was no one left to look after Louise at home.
>
> They both received the maximum Centrelink age pension and had been quite comfortable with this level of income.

The family looked at several homes and found one that looked suitable. It had several double rooms for couples and was asking for an RAD of $450,000 each.

Due to their level of assets, if Charlie and Louise had entered at the same time they each would have to pay the full RAD. After receiving financial advice, Louise moved in first and Charlie followed later.

Because of this staggered entry the family home was regarded as an exempt asset (because Charlie was still living there) and it was not assessed when Centrelink looked at their assets. As a result Louise was assessed as having negligible assets, became a low-means resident and didn't have to make an accommodation payment. Charlie entered care two weeks later and agreed to pay the RAD of $450,000.

As a result they paid lower aged-care fees and received higher Centrelink age pensions.

Lesson: Never underestimate the value and benefits of investing in good financial advice.

Strategy 11 — spend cash

Cash and investments are also included in the assets and income assessment, so one way of reducing the level of Mum's means tested amount is to spend some cash. She could consider making improvements to the family home. This could have the added advantage of increasing its value and thus preserving more of her finances (albeit in the form of property instead of cash) as well as reducing her assessable assets.

Alternatively she might subscribe to the SKI theory —

Spending the Kids' Inheritance. Unfulfilled dreams or holidays are fun ways of reducing cash or investment levels. If Mum wants to consider this option she could think about doing it earlier in life. By reducing her assets level before she reaches pension age, she could also potentially be increasing her pension entitlements when the time comes.

These strategies can be very effective when Mum's assets only just exceed the threshold for the pension assets test. If she didn't reduce her assets, she wouldn't be eligible for the pension or other benefits.

PART 4

Checklists
Resources
Glossary of terms

Top Tips

- **myagedcare.gov.au** has answers to almost every question about the aged-care system.
- Copy the checklists in preparation for visiting homes.
- Go to the relevant website to gather more information, especially those of your preferred homes.

Chapter 20:
Resources

This section of the book is a reference library almost. It lists sources of information on just about every aspect of aged care for easy access. You will find:

- Checklists for finding a home and for neglect
- All the ACAT contact details throughout Australia
- Lists of placement services throughout Australia
- Online sources for finding homes
- Resources for carers, dementia and the many faces of Centrelink
- State- and territory-based resources for advocacy, guardianship and more
- Glossary of terms used throughout the book.

Checklists

There are four lists given here and the first three provide details to look out for you are checking out homes before deciding on your preferred one. The first is a broad outline of the process of getting into a home, the second is for use when visiting any residential homes and the third list gives additional criteria that are specific to dementia homes. The last is a list for checking for neglect or mistreatment.

These are designed to help set your own priorities. If Mum is moving into a dementia unit, her needs will be different from those if she is moving into permanent care. If she is only going for respite care, you may have to accept that some of these criteria may not be an option.

Before you visit, photocopy the lists making one for each home you are going to see. Then mark the important criteria with a highlight pen so that they stand out when you are going around. After you leave the home take a few minutes to make notes about both the positives and the negatives. When you get home you will then have an objective, factual document to use in your decision-making.

General homes checklist

This list is in alphabetic order for ease of use. You will see that each section only has short phrases for each point. These are meant to be triggers for you to think about. They are also intended to be read as questions. For example, under Bedroom and Bathroom we have listed 'Bring your own furniture'. This is meant to be read as 'can we bring some of Mum's own furniture to put in her room?'

Process for finding a home

- Contact myagedcare to discuss Mum's needs
- Arrange for an ACAT assessment
- Make copies of the ACAT approval to take when you visit homes
- Create a list of homes in Mum's preferred are from the myagedcare website's search page
- Estimate Mum's fees and charges using the fees estimator page on the myagedcare website
- Contact your chosen homes, visit and submit an application
- Undertake as much preparation at home as you can while you wait for an offer
- After you have negotiated a place complete the financial forms and submit them to Centrelink or get professional help with them
- Book a moving van for the day and move in!
- Understand and sign the Resident's Agreement

(Derived from the Department of Social Services' *Five steps to entry into an aged care home*.)

General Home Checklist

Home ....

Activities
List up on noticeboard
Activities of interest
Mentally stimulating activities
Social events / outings

Bedroom & Bathroom
Smell
Clean
Light and airy
Temperature — local controls
Windows can be opened
Outlook or view
Lockable drawer / cupboard
Sufficient storage
Distance to lounge or dining rooms
Bring own furniture
Bathroom privacy
Safety rails in the bathroom
Computer connection

Care
Staff to resident ratios
Staff happy or hassled
Staff respectful of residents
Staff you can understand
Keep your own doctor
Doctors visit regularly
Family can help in caring
Number / type of night staff
Registered nurse on every shift

Culture / religion
Staff who speak your language
Other residents of your culture
Culturally appropriate meals
Culturally appropriate activities
Practice your own religion
Transport to your place of worship

Environment

Quiet neighbourhood

Sufficient parking

Parks / open spaces nearby

Building in good repair

Gardens well kept

External lighting / security

Local facilities nearby

Facilities

Newspapers delivered

Mail — sending and receiving

Computers connected to the internet

Multiple lounges

Quiet area — no TV

Non-denominational chapel

Residents' garden

Hairdresser

Podiatrist

Physio

Occupational therapist

Interior

Smell

Temperature

Lighting

Receptionist

Silence or chatter

Wheelchair friendly

Comfortable furniture

Pleasant dining room

Toilets near lounges

Handrails in corridors

House Rules

Alcohol and smoking

Pets

Sexual activity

Getting up / bedtime hours

Showering times

Cleaning frequency

Bed made

Laundry times / frequency

Meal times

Management / Legal
Certificates on view
Certification certificate up to date
Accreditation certificate up to date
Food Handlers Licence up to date
Residents and Relatives Group

Meals
Frequency of menu change
Foods Mum likes
Balanced and nutritious
Cooked on the premises
Special diets catered for
Wine / beer with meals
Meals in your room
Morning / afternoon tea

Resident's Agreement
Amount of deposit
Methods of paying the deposit
Fees — how much, when payable
Extra services — costs
What is not covered?
Mum wants to leave
They ask Mum to leave
Complaints procedures

Visitors
Anyone, any time
Private lounges for guests
Stay for a meal
Drinks or snacks

Ask for a copy of
Resident's Agreement
Application form and process

Dementia Home Checklist

Home ....

- Do the staff listen and ask for information?
- Does it feel friendly and welcoming?
- Is there somewhere to sit quietly and privately?
- Can you to come and help Mum with showering and feeding?
- Can Mum keep her own doctor
- Are you satisfied with the medical and specialist services?
- What is the medication policy?
- What are the fire procedures?
- Are you satisfied with the range of activities?
- Can outings, overnight stays and holidays with family members be arranged?
- Do the other residents appear well cared for?
- Have the care and nursing staff had specialist dementia training?
- Can increased needs be catered for in the future?
- Is it obvious how to get to a toilet from the public areas?
- Are residents' different cultural needs met?
- Are objects that residents are likely to bump into or trip over, in safe places?
- Would it be clear to the resident where to go to if they needed help?
- Are the furnishings, particularly in their room, subtle and home-like so they are not too busy or distracting?
- If a resident is lost, are there objects or landmarks that would help them work out where they are?
- Is there a safe, sun-protected outdoor space?
- What are the external security arrangements to prevent residents wandering away and getting lost?

Neglect Checklist

Does the home smell?

Check the resident:
- Are they wearing their glasses? If not, ask where they are.
- Are they wearing their hearing aid(s)? Is the battery dead? Is it turned on?
- Do they have their teeth in? If not, ask where they are.
- Are their nails long and jagged or short and clean?
- Do they smell? Are they wet or messy?
- Is their hair combed? Are they wearing clean clothes?
- Ask about carers scolding or yelling at them.

Check the meal trays:
- If the resident is diabetic, is there a note stating this? Is there a sugar bowl
- on the tray?
- What does the food look like? Is it hot?
- Check the trolley as it returns to the kitchen. Are meals eaten or untouched?

Check the resident's room:
- Is there a water jug with either a glass or a straw? Is the water fresh?
- Can they reach the call bell/buzzer?
- Does the bell work? Is it plugged in?
- How long before it is answered?

How many residents does each carer have to feed?
- They should be feeding a maximum of four at the one time.

Check the activity calendar:
- Are all the listed activities actually taking place?

How many residents have bruises or bandages?
- Does it seem to be a disproportionately high number?

How many residents are parked in their wheelchairs in hallways or their rooms?

How many air beds are there in the home?
- Air beds may be used to treat bedsores. Is there a disproportionate number, possibly indicating that residents are not being turned often enough or the nutrition is poor?

(Adapted from **agedcarecrisis.com**)

Aged Care Assessment Teams

These are taken from the DSS website (with permission) and are correct at the time of writing. They are listed alphabetically by state or territory and teams are listed alphabetically by town/region within each group.

NSW — Sydney

Canberra	02 6207 9977
Auburn	02 9749 0379
Bankstown	1800 455 511
Blacktown	02 9881 288
Blue Mountains	1800 013 101
Camperdown	1800 556 533
Illawarra	1300 792 755
Kogarah — St Georges	02 9553 3000
Liverpool/Fairfield	1800 455 511
Lower North Shore	02 9926 8705
Northern Beaches	02 9926 8705
Penrith, Hawkesbury	1800 013 101
Randwick/Botany	02 9369 0400
Ryde	02 9858 7782
Sydney Inner West — Canterbury	1800 556 533
Sydney Inner West — Concord	1800 556 533
Sutherland	02 9540 7175
Westmead	02 9845 6903
Wingecarribee	02 4861 8000
Wyoming/Central Coast	02 4304 0700

NSW- Regional

Armidale	02 6776 9688
Balranald	02 5020 0194
Bathurst	02 6332 8963
Bega Valley	02 6495 7294
Broken Hill	08 8080 1663
Clarence Valley	02 6641 8270
Cooma-Snowy	02 6455 3202
Cootamundra	02 6940 1111
Corowa	02 6033 1340
Dareton	02 5021 7200
Deniliquin	03 5882 2900
Dubbo	02 6841 8529
Eurobodalla	02 4474 1570
Finley	03 5883 3627
Griffith/Murrumbidgee	02 6961 8080
Goulburn	02 4823 7890
Hastings-Macleay	02 6588 2875
Holbrook	02 6036 2787
Hunter Rural	02 4936 3215
Hunter Urban	02 4985 5700
Leeton	02 6953 1251
Lithgow	02 6350 2506
Manning/Great Lakes	02 6515 1800
Narrabri	02 6799 2002
Orange	02 6393 3500
Parkes	02 6861 2555
Richmond Valley	02 6620 6222
Tamworth	02 6767 8300
Tweed Valley	07 5506 7590
Walgett	02 6828 6000

West Wyalong	02 6972 2122
Wingecarribbee	02 4861 8000
Young, Boorowa, Harden	02 6382 8444

Northern Territory

Alice Springs Remote	08 8951 6744
Darwin	08 8922 7393
Katherine	08 8973 8503

Queensland

Brisbane Hospital	07 3624 1203
Brisbane South	07 3275 5411
Bayside	07 3488 4231
Caboolture	07 5433 8300
Cairns	07 4226 6446
Central West	07 4650 4000
Chermside	1300 658 252
Gold Coast	1300 130 143
Innisfail	07 4061 5401
Ipswich — West Moreton	07 3413 5850
Mackay	07 4885 7777
Mareeba, Tablelands	07 4092 9121
Mount Isa	07 4744 7153
Nambour	07 5470 6731
Pine Rivers	1300 658 252
Rockhampton	07 4920 6900
Roma	07 4624 2977
South West (Toowoomba)	07 4699 8901
Townsville	07 4799 9050
Wide Bay, Burnett, Fraser Coast	07 4122 8733

South Australia

Adelaide — Southern Office	1300 296 738
Adelaide Hills	08 8393 1831
Barossa	08 8563 8544
Flinders & Far North	1300 760 177
Kangaroo Island	08 8553 4266
Lower Eyre Peninsula	08 8683 2077
Lower North	08 8842 6500
Lower South East	08 8721 1460
Mid-North	08 8638 4693
Murray Mallee	08 8535 6800
Riverland	08 8580 4195
Southern Fleurieu	08 8552 0600
Upper South East	08 8762 8160
Whyalla	08 8648 8500
Yorke Peninsula	08 8823 0274

Tasmania

Launceston	03 6336 4144
North West	03 6429 8400
Southern	03 6222 7274

Victoria — Melbourne

Bundoora	03 9495 3109
Caulfield	03 9076 6314
Eastern Metro	03 9881 1875
Heidelberg	03 9496 2489
Kew	03 9816 0566
North West	03 8387 2129
Western	03 8345 1246

Victoria — Regional

Bairnsdale	1800 242 696
Barwon Region	03 5279 2246
Grampians	03 5320 3740
Korumburra	1800 242 696
Mildura	03 5022 5444
Morwell	1800 242 696
Sale	1800 242 696
South West	03 5561 9351
Shepparton	03 5823 6000
Wangaratta	03 5723 2000
Warragul	1800 242 696

Western Australia

Armadale	08 9391 2250
Bentley	08 9334 3770
Broome	08 9192 0333
Fremantle	08 9431 2673

Great Southern	**08 9842 7580**
Goldfields	**08 9080 5772**
Mandurah	**08 9599 4517**
Mid-West	**08 9956 2310**
Narrogin	**08 9881 0385**
Nedlands	**08 9346 2078**
Northam Wheatbelt	**08 9690 1318**
Osborne Park	**08 9346 8111**
Perth	**08 9370 9900**
Pilbara	**08 9174 1081**
South West	**08 9722 4300**
Swan	**08 9347 5423**

Placement services

New South Wales

Aged Care Admissions Services	Killara	02 9449 7331
Aged Care Placement Services	Sans Souci	1300 882 808
Health and Aged Assist	Ryde	1300 784 781
Machado Aged Care	Wareemba	02 9713 5589
Shire Aged Care Placement Specialists	Caringbah	1300 883 816
Third Age Matters	Narrabundah	1300 350 093

Queensland

Aged Care Assistance Placement Consultancy	Samford	07 3289 2431
Aged Care Guidance	Brisbane	07 3142 3778
Health and Aged Assist	Coolangatta	1300 730 074
Heather Hill Pathways	Toowong	1300 227 949
Home & Residential Care Consultancy	Everton Park	1300 158 884
Sunshine Coast Aged Care Placement	Moffat Beach	07 5491 4470

South Australia

Aged Care Directions	Highbury	**08 8337 9851**
Aged Care Planning	Mitcham	**08 8272 1846**
AJ Case Consulting	Athelstone	**0413 209 996**
Bernadette Stockwell	Glengowrie	**08 8294 4666**
Senexus Aged Care Solutions	Prospect	**08 8344 1991**
Seniors Pathway	Frewville	**08 8379 5006**

Victoria

ACP Placements	Ringwood	**03 9720 3883**
Aged Care Connect	Kew	**1300 884 850**
Aged Care Counselling	Emerald	**0418 574 098**
Aged Care Placement	South Yarra	**1300 134 783**
Health and Aged Assist	Mt Waverley	**1300 784 781**
Help@Hand Aged Care Placements	Black Rock	**03 9598 7717**
Homecare Relief	Malvern	**03 9357 4001**
Into Aged Care	Camberwell	**0438 598 831**
Joseph Palmer & Sons	Melbourne	**03 9601 6800**
Millennium	Mont Albert	**1300 755 702**
moveU by tlc	Caulfield North	**0411 757 185**
Ninox Advisory	Docklands	**1300 064 669**
One Care Australia	Blackburn	**1800 663 227**
Seamless Transitions	Melbourne	**0419 336 603**
Signpost Aged Care Services	Hawthorn	**1800 744 676**
Tender Living Care	Kew East	**1300 889 356**

Western Australia

Aged Care & Retirement Placement Services	Subiaco	0433 796 512
Empathy Care	Perth	08 9291 3064
Jan Desmond Aged Care Consultant	Willeton	08 9354 2082
Relacs Placement Consultants	Mount Lawley	08 6143 2565

Homes in Australia

- Aged Care Central: **myagedcare.gov.au/welcome-my-aged-care**

- Aged Care Online: **agedcareonline.com.au/residential-aged-care**

- DPS Guide: **agedcareguide.com.au/residential-aged-care-australia.asp**

- SRS in Victoria: **docs.health.vic.gov.au/docs/doc/A-to-Z-Listing-of-SRS-Facilities**

- SRS in South Australia: **seniors.asn.au/centric/residential_aged_care/supported_residential_facilities.jsp**

- For the low-income and homeless: **wintringham.org.au** or **03 9034 4824**

Independent Online Resources

Aged Care Crisis	Information and support	**agedcarecrisis.com**
Aged Care Guide	Directory	**agedcareguide.com.au**
Aged Care Online	Directory	**agedcareonline.com.au**
Australian Health Directory	Directory	**healthdirectory.com.au/fts/search?ftky=health+directory&section=health**
Eden Alternative	Alternative aged care model and directory	**edeninoz.com.au**
Facebook	Aged care groups and information	**facebook.com**

National Resources

Centrelink

Home page		humanservices.gov.au/customer/information/centrelink-website?utm_id=7
Age Pension & Retirement	13 23 00	humanservices.gov.au/customer/services/centrelink/age-pension?utm_id=7
Carer Adjustment Payment	13 27 17	dss.gov.au/our-responsibilities/disability-and-carers/benefits-payments/carer-adjustment-payment
Customer Relations	1800 050 004	
Health Care Card		humanservices.gov.au/customer/services/centrelink/health-care-card?utm_id=7
Carer Allowance		humanservices.gov.au/customer/services/centrelink/carer-allowance?utm_id=7

Carer Resources

Carers gateway		**carergateway.gov.au/counselling**
myagedcare	**1800 200 422**	**myagedcare.gov.au/**
Carers Australia	**1800 242 636**	**carersaustralia.com.au**
Commonwealth Respite and Carelink Centres	**1800 052 222**	
Carer Allowance		**humanservices.gov.au/customer/services/centrelink/carer-allowance?utm_id=7**

Dementia Support

National Helpline	**1800 100 500**	**fightdementia.org.au/services/helpline**
Alzheimer's Australia	**1800 100 500**	**fightdementia.org.au/**
Dementia Care Australia (DCA)	**03 9727 2744**	**dementiacareaustralia.com**

Other Departments

Aged Care Assessment Teams	1800 200 422	myagedcare.gov.au/eligibility-and-assessment/acat-assessments
Aged Care Complaints	1800 200 422	agedcarecomplaints.gov.au
Australian Aged Care Quality Agency	1800 288 025	aacqua.gov.au
Commonwealth Ombudsman Services	1300 362 072	ombudsman.gov.au/pages/making-a-complaint/
Department of Health	1800 020 103	health.gov.au/
Department of Veterans Affairs (DVA)	13 32 54 or 1800 555 254	dva.gov.au/
Medicare	13 20 11	humanservices.gov.au/customer/information/welcome-medicare-customers-website?utm_id=9
Tax Office	13 28 65	ato.gov.au/individuals/

Telephone Book

The *White Pages for Business and Government* lists many resources on the Advice and Assistance pages near the front of the book.

State Resources

ACT

Advocacy Services ACT Disability, Aged & Care Advocacy Services	02 6242 5060	adacas.org.au
Carers ACT	1800 242 636	carersact.org.au/
Council for the Ageing (COTA)	02 6282 3777	cota-act.org.au
Elder Abuse Prevention Information Line	02 6205 3535	communityservices.act.gov.au/wac/ageing/elder_abuse_prevention__and__assistance
Guardianship Public Advocate of the ACT	02 6207 0707	publicadvocate.act.gov.au
Public Trustee for ACT	02 6207 9800	publictrustee.act.gov.au
Health Department ACT Health	13 22 81	health.act.gov.au/c/health
Ombudsman	1300 362 072	ombudsman.act.gov.au

New South Wales

Advocacy Services The Aged Care Rights Service	1800 424 079	tars.com.au
Carers NSW	1800 242 636	carersnsw.asn.au/
Council for the Ageing (COTA)	02 9286 3860 1800 449 102	cotansw.com.au
Elder Abuse	1800 628 221	
Guardianship NSW Trustee and Guardian	1300 364 103	tag.nsw.gov.au
Health Department	02 9391 9000	health.nsw.gov.au
Ombudsman Rural callers	02 9286 1000 1800 451 524	ombo.nsw.gov.au Online form

Northern Territory

Advocacy Services Aged & Disability Rights Team (Darwin) Centacare (Alice Springs)	1800 812 953 1800 354 550	dcls.org.au
Carers NT Rural callers	1800 242 636 08 89 444 888	carersnt.asn.au/
Council for the Ageing (COTA)	08 8941 1004	cotant.org

Elder Abuse
NT Health Services (Darwin)	08 8999 2809	health.nt.gov.au/
NT Police	13 14 44	

Guardianship
Office of Public Trustee
Darwin	08 8999 7271	nt.gov.au/justice/
Alice Springs	08 8951 5493	pubtrust/

Health Department
Department of Health and Families	08 8999 2400	nt.gov.au/health/

Ombudsman   1800 806 380   ombudsman.nt.gov.au

Queensland

Advocacy Services
Queensland Aged, Disability and Advocacy	1800 818 338	qada.org.au

Carers Qld	1800 242 636	carersqld.asn.au/

Council for the Ageing (COTA)	07 3138 1146	cotaq.org.au

Elder Abuse
Elder Abuse Prevention Unit	07 3250 1955	
Rural callers	1300 651 192	

Guardianship

Adult Guardian	1300 653 187	publicguardian.qld.gov.au/adult-guardian
Public Trustee	1300 360 044	pt.qld.gov.au
Public Advocate	07 3224 7424	justice.qld.gov.au/justice-services/guardianship/public-advocate

Health Department	07 3234 0111	health.qld.gov.au

Ombudsman
Brisbane	07 3005 7000	ombudsman.qld.gov.au
Rural callers	1800 068 908	

South Australia

Advocacy Services
Aged Rights Advocacy Services	1800 700 600	sa.agedrights.asn.au

Carers SA	1800 242 636	carers-sa.asn.au/

Council for the Ageing (COTA)	08 8232 0422	cotasa.org.au/default.aspx
Rural callers	1800 182 324	

Elder Abuse
Aged Rights
Advocacy Services Adelaide	08 8232 5377	sa.agedrights.asn.au
Rural callers	1800 700 600	

Guardianship

Office of Public Advocate		opa.sa.gov.au/
Adelaide	08 8342 8200	
Rural callers	1800 066 969	
Public Trustee		publictrustee.sa.gov.au/
Adelaide	08 8226 9200	
Rural callers	1800 673 119	

Health Department	08 8226 6000	sahealth.sa.gov.au

Ombudsman		ombudsman.sa.gov.au
Adelaide	08 8226 8699	
Rural callers	1800 182 150	

Tasmania

Advocacy Services

Advocacy Tasmania	03 6224 2240	advocacytasmania.org.au/

Carers Tasmania	1800 242 636	carerstas.org/

Council for the Ageing (COTA)	03 6228 1897	cotatas.org

Elder Abuse

Department of Health and Human Services	1300 135 513	dhhs.tas.gov.au/
Aged Rights Advocacy Service	03 6224 2240	agedrights.asn.au

Guardianship

Office of Public Guardian	03 6165 3444	publicguardian.tas.gov.au
Public Trustee —		
Hobart	03 6235 5200	publictrustee.tas.gov.au
Launceston	03 6335 3400	
Burnie	03 6430 3600	
Devonport	03 6430 3600	

Health Department

Department of Health and Human Services	1300 135 513	dhhs.tas.gov.au
Ombudsman	1800 001 170	ombudsman.tas.gov.au/

Victoria

Advocacy Services

Elders Rights Advocacy	03 9602 3066	era.asn.au
Free call except from mobiles	1800 700 600	

Carers Victoria	1800 242 636	carersvictoria.org.au/
Council for the Ageing (COTA)	03 9654 4443	cotavic.org.au

Elder Abuse

Seniors Information Victoria	1800 200 422	myagedcare.gov.au
Seniors Rights Victoria	03 9654 4443	cotavic.org.au/action-advocacy/information/seniors-rights-victoria/

Guardianship		
Office of the Public Advocate	1300 309 337 03 9667 6466	publicadvocate.vic.gov.au
State Trustees	1300 138 672	statetrustees.com.au
Health Department Mobile users	1300 650 172 03 9096 9000	health.vic.gov.au
Ombudsman Rural callers	03 9613 6222 1800 806 314	ombudsman.vic.gov.au

Western Australia

Advocacy Services Advocare		
Perth callers Rural callers	08 9479 7566 1800 655 566	advocare.org.au
Carers WA	08 9472 0104	carerswa.asn.au/
Council for the Ageing (COTA)	08 9321 2133	cotawa.org.au/
Elder Abuse Advocare		
Perth callers Rural callers	08 9479 7566 1800 655 566	advocare.org.au
Guardianship Office of the Public Advocate	1300 858 455	publicadvocate.wa.gov.au
Public Trustee	1300 746 116	publictrustee.wa.gov.au

Health Department	08 9222 4222	health.wa.gov.au
Ombudsman	08 9220 7555	ombudsman.wa.gov.au
Rural callers	**1800 117 000**	

Glossary of Terms

AACQA
See Australian Aged Care Quality Agency

ACAS — Aged Care Assessment Services
The term used in Victoria for ACAT.

ACAT — Aged Care Assessment Team
Aged Care Assessment Teams (ACAT) help older people and their carers assess what kind of care will best meet their needs. ACATs provide information on suitable care options and undertake the assessment that will provide the approval paperwork for access to a Home Care Package or residential care.

Accommodation payment
Accommodation payment is a contribution to the cost of accommodation which is used to maintain the home. The amount you will have to pay is determined from the level of your assets. See RAD and RAC.

ACCR — Aged Care Client Record

This is the central client record which contains client details (and carer or representative details), details about assessments, the support plan and information about services that a client receives.

Accreditation

Accreditation is the formal process of acknowledging that a residential aged-care home is operating to the mandatory standards set by the Australian Aged Care Quality Agency in accordance with the *Aged Care Act 1997*. It defines high quality care within a framework of continuous improvement and checks.

Administrator

An administrator or financial manager is responsible for making financial decisions or giving advice for adults who do not have legal capacity to make these decisions for themselves. Each state and territory has a Guardianship Board which has powers to appoint a guardian or administrator.

Advanced care directive

This is a document in which a person expresses their wishes and preferences for their comfort, dignity and treatment during critical and terminal illnesses when they can no longer communicate themselves. Also called a living will.

Aged Care Client Record

See ACCR.

Aged Care Complaints

Aged Care Complaints is a government scheme that provides a free independent service to help residents and their families resolve complaints about an aged-care provider whether they are an at-home provider or a residential home.

Ageing-in-place

A residential home offering ageing-in-place is providing all levels of care from at-home care through to high and secure dementia care. If a low-care resident deteriorates to the point that they now need high care, they have the option to receive the extended care without having to move homes.

Assessment

This is an evaluation undertaken to identify a person's capacities and limitations in relation to their personal care and safety. The resulting approval paperwork is needed to access a Home Care Package or a residential home.

Australian Aged Care Quality Agency — AACQA

This is an independent agency established by the federal government to manage the accreditation process. It provides assistance to improve service quality through education and training, information dissemination and identification of best practice.

Care plan

A dynamic document that comprises a statement of the resident's problems which have been determined during an assessment. It will have resident-centred goals together with strategies, interventions or actions intended to help the resident achieve or maintain those goals.

CDC
Consumer-directed care. This is the philosophy behind the management and delivery of Home Care Packages — and from 2017 residential homes as well. It aims to give the consumer control over what services they receive and when, who provides them and how they spend their budget.

Certification
Certification focuses on the physical facilities and infrastructure of a home and is based on the Building Code of Australia. It includes regulations about safety, privacy, access, mobility, heating and cooling, lighting and ventilation and security.

CHSP — Commonwealth Home Support Programme
One of the two government-subsidised at-home care programs.

Commonwealth Respite and Carelink Centres
These are a national network of centres which facilitate access to information, respite care and other support appropriate to carers' needs and circumstances, and the needs of the people they care for.

Consumer Directed Care
See CDC.

Continuing care resident
Anyone who entered permanent residential aged care before 1 July 2014.

Daily care fees

Residents of aged-care homes will be asked to pay a daily fee for the care they receive. This includes a basic daily fee for at-home care residents as well as residential care and a daily income tested fee or a means tested fee for some residents depending on their income. Residents who receive a full means tested pension cannot be asked to pay an income tested fee or a means-tested fee.

DAC

Daily accommodation contribution.

DAP

Daily accommodation payment.

DHS

Department of Human Services.

DON (Director of Nursing)

A DON oversees all nursing staff in a residential home and is responsible for formulating nursing policies and monitoring the quality of care delivered, as well as the home's compliance with government regulations relating to nursing care.

DSS

Department of Social Services.

DVA

Department of Veterans Affairs.

Enduring Power of Attorney (Financial)
This is a legal document appointing a person to make legally-binding financial decisions on behalf of another person in the event that they can no longer make those decisions for themselves.

Enduring Power of Attorney (Medical Treatment)
This is a legal document appointing a person to make medical treatment decisions on behalf of another person in the event that they can legally no longer make those decisions for themselves.

Extra-services home
An extra-services home provides significantly higher standards of accommodation and services to residents for which an additional, extra-services fee is paid.

High-level care
Nursing care together with personal and domestic care which may be provided in your own home but more often in a residential care home.

Home Care Agreement
A legally binding agreement between the provider and consumer of a Home Care Package.

ITF
Income tested fee.

LITO
Low income tax offset.

Living will
This is a document designed for a person to express their wishes and preferences for their comfort, dignity and treatment during critical and terminal illnesses when they can no longer communicate themselves. Also called an advanced care directive.

Low-level care
A supported care environment which provides domestic and personal care either in your own home or in a residential care home.

MAC
The myagedcare website and call centre at **myagedcare.gov.au**. This is the central and only access point to all aged-care services across Australia.

MPIR
Maximum permissible interest rate.

MTA
Means tested amount.

Multi-purpose services
Multi-purpose services are designed specifically for rural and regional areas, bringing together a range of health and aged-care services (for example, hospitals, community services, family support and aged care services).

myagedcare — MAC
The internet-based gateway to all aged-care services at **myagedcare.gov.au**.

NSAF — National Screening and Assessment Form
This now replaces the ACCR.

Palliative care
The practice of managing symptoms toward the end of life as fully as possible so they are tolerable for the individual. It also supports the person and the family to a comfortable death.

Pensioner
A person is classed as a pensioner if they either receive a means tested pension or benefit from Centrelink or the DVA or hold a current Pensioner Concession Card.

Personal Care Assistant — PCA
Staff who help residents perform personal activities such as bathing, toileting and dressing.

Power of Attorney
A Power of Attorney is a legal document in which a person appoints someone else, usually a trusted family member or friend, to act as their agent. It conveys the authority to deal with and manage their property and other financial affairs. There are several types of powers of attorney.

Public Advocate
These are independent statutory offices of each state or territory government. Their role is to provide assistance to people who may need help with decision making particularly in areas like guardianship and advocacy. They can also be appointed as a person's guardian if there is nobody else who can fill this role.

RAC
Refundable accommodation contribution.

RAD
Refundable accommodation deposit.

Resident's Agreement
A resident's agreement is a legal document that sets out the rights and obligations of both the resident and the aged-care home. The agreement should cover a variety of issues relating to service provision, fees and charges, the rights and responsibilities of the home, the resident and any extra services.

Sanctions
Sanctions are actions imposed against a care-provider for non-compliance with the standards under the *Aged Care Act 1997*. This applies to both at-home care and residential homes.

SAPTO
Senior Australian and Pensioner's Tax Offset.

SRS — Supported Residential Services
These are private care homes which operate outside the government's aged-care system. These are usually state-based and regulated at that level. They are not subsidised.

State Trustees
See Public Advocate.

Transition care
Transition care is interim temporary care services after a stay in hospital and before either returning home or going to residential care.

Trust Companies
See Public Advocate.

Will
This is a legal document which defines how a person wants their estate to be distributed after they die. Without a will there is no guarantee that those wishes can be carried out. Dying without a will is called intestate and there is a legally-defined structure for who inherits.

About the Author

Val Nigol

Val is a financial adviser and accountant who, for over thirty years, has been creating financial optimisation strategies for individuals and families facing, or already in, retirement and later life. Residential aged care brings specific financial concerns and criteria and Val is one of very few authorities in this niche area. His unique contribution to *Aged Care* is the up-to-date explanations of the complex rules and costs, together with mix-and-match strategies for families to consider when they are faced with moving a loved one into care.

Val has over fifteen years' experience in this specialist sector and is well qualified to write this book:

- Master of Business Administration
- Fellow of the Institute of Chartered Accountants in Australia
- Member of Financial Planning Chapter of the Institute of Chartered Accountants in Australia
- Registered Tax Agent

Acknowledgements

Some years ago I recognised that my clients were increasingly seeking advice around residential aged care and that there was no how-to book to help them. That was the catalyst for the first edition of *Aged Care Homes, the complete Australian guide* in 2008.

This new edition reflects the wider world of at-home care as well and I am indebted to Anthea Wynn for her research, writing, editing and recrafting my ponderous thoughts particularly on the financials.

I gratefully acknowledge the contributions made by the many professionals who willingly and enthusiastically gave us their time and expertise. In particular, Cynthia's 20+ years of aged care nursing experience has been our guiding light. Also to Ron Carroll for his understanding of the recent changes and Stephanie King for her expertise and proof-reading.

I am equally appreciative of all those people whose personal experiences have enlivened our understanding and the text with their stories including those others who wish to remain anonymous — you will know who we mean.

I additionally commemorate those who contributed initially but who have passed in the meantime, namely Sadie, Cynthia, Graham, Athole and Margery.

I also gratefully acknowledge the following organisations

for the use of their copyright material: Aged Care Connect, Aged Care Crisis, Alzheimer's Australia, Australian Bureau of Statistics, Australian Institute of Health and Welfare, Department of Human Services, and Department of Social Services and Department of Health.